Coaching Issues & Dilemmas:

Character Building
Through Sport Participation

Carol L. Alberts
Hofstra University

Photographs by:
Luke DeLalio, The Long Island Herald and Jennifer Baker, Hofstra
University

Address orders to: AAHPERD Publications, P.O. Box 385, Oxon
Hill, MD 20750-0385, call 1-800-321-0789, or order on line at
www.aahperd.org/naspe.
Order Stock No 304-10270.

Printed in the United States of America.

ISBN 0-88314-902-8

TABLE OF CONTENTS

FOREWORD

We require our driver education teachers and librarians to be certified in order to be employed as teachers for our children. No such requirement exists for coaches. In many school systems, any full-time employee, including a custodian or teacher's aide, can coach if he or she successfully passes a first aid course. Yet we know that training a football team in 100-degree heat can cause a player's death from heat stroke and that someone who doesn't understand the principles of weight training can cause athletes to suffer joint injuries. We know that a coach's words, if they are misused in the psychologically stressful environment of sport, can destroy self-esteem, confidence, and the motivation to succeed. We also know that, outside of school, well-meaning but unprepared parents face extraordinary challenges trying to guide their children in the pressure-packed world of youth sports. Yet, despite knowing all this, we often allow the least-trained and sometimes least-questioned teachers to be sport coaches.

When schools and leagues do provide training for coaches, they concentrate on physiological information and the X's and O's. The moral basics are forgotten: treat every child with respect and dignity, show respect for officials, use constructive criticism, do not teach anyone to intentionally hurt others, show remorse for actions or words that are hurtful, be truthful, and accept responsibility. Sure, we know what these words mean. However, when we do not take the time to analyze right and wrong in specific sport situations, or when we fail to practice introspection and just continue to coach the way we were coached, we simply do not recognize ethical and unethical behaviors.

We know that teams behave in ways that emulate the values taught by their coaches. *Coaching Issues and Dilemmas: Character Building Through Sport Participation* is a book that will help every coach at every level of experience identify opportunities to teach values and to demand that players exhibit good character and sportsmanship. The author makes the coach take a more critical look at methods and behaviors that are seldom questioned. A particular strength of the text is a comprehensive treatment of the most difficult situations encountered by coaches, from dealing with discipline and enraged parents to starting freshmen over seniors.

During youth and adolescence, our children appear to ignore the advice of parents and teachers while they listen to every word of peers who know little or nothing. During these critical developmental periods, the adult who still remains highly influential is often the sport coach. What should we demand of these leaders? If we are coaches, what should we demand of ourselves? Read on and be better for it.

—Donna A. Lopiano, Ph.D.
Executive Director
Women's Sports Foundation

ACKNOWLEDGEMENTS

I have read many authors' acknowledgements, and must confess that I have sometimes thought, "enough already" or "did they do anything themselves?" Now I understand. As a coach, teacher, and teacher/coach educator, I knew I had something to say, but did not see myself as a writer. It has been a learning journey, and the lessons are not all that different from those I learned on the sports fields.

So, my first acknowledgement is to those who encouraged and inspired me to take the challenge and helped me frame what I had to say. Janet Miller, Elizabeth Ellsworth, Kathy Oitzinger, and Arthur and Lyn Dobrin provided guidance, encouragement, and helpful insights all along the way. I also want to thank Ed Frankel, Peg Harned, Diane Heckman, and Joan Beder for their valuable input on earlier drafts of the manuscript.

Without the help of my brother, Mark, I think the manuscript would still be in machine language in some forever-lost computer file. Also deserving recognition are the students at Hofstra who helped with research and photographs. I thank Sasha Blake and Heather Hogan for their behind-the-scenes work and many trips to the library and Jennifer Baker for her photographs.

I would also like to extend a special thanks to Brenda Bredemeir and Notre Dame's Mendelson Center for Sport, Character, and Community for including me as part of their team and supporting me throughout this endeavor. Also, thanks to Luke DeLalio of the Long Island Herald for allowing me access to their sport photograph archives and for taking time out of his busy schedule to photograph for me.

And to my family and friends, Sue Smith, Barbara Intrieri, and Jane Sterling who, whether they wanted to or not, lived through my trials and tribulations of becoming an author, I am indebted and most appreciative. Finally, without my friend and editor, Barbara Grey, I don't think I would be writing this acknowledgement. Her clarity of thinking, editorial skill, patience, quick turn-around time, and unconditional support made me a writer. How do you thank someone for that?

—Carol L. Alberts, Ed.D.
Hofstra University

INTRODUCTION

Americans are struggling to reidentify family roles and the family unit. They are concerned about increasing violence and the prevalence of society's "win-at-all-costs" mentality. There is a strong feeling that basic values are changing. Many feel that the picture for the future is not optimistic. The long-term view is that the values passed down from today's adults will be the values that our grandchildren inherit. However, the amount of time young people spend with adults is diminishing. How will essential personal and social values be transmitted?

Coaches Can Affect Players' Attitudes and Beliefs

One place where there is potential for influencing character development is in sport. Sport plays a significant role in family and leisure time and is an integral part of our education system. Most Americans believe that sport participation builds character. Americans value the positive qualities of successful athletes. They feel that athletes develop these qualities from their competitive sport participation. Thus, athletic participation is viewed as training for success in life. However, the same "win-at-all-costs" mentality pervasive in society is also prevalent on our nation's playing fields. There is a need to reexamine the purpose of school and youth sports, and to ask these questions: What are our children learning on the sports fields? What kinds of influences do coaches have on the development of values, character, and basic social skills?

The National Association for Sport and Physical Education (NASPE) has facilitated a national consensus about standards for coaches that will ensure that individuals that meet these standards will be able to provide appropriate developmental experiences for athletes. *Coaching Issues & Dilemmas: Character Building Through Sport Participation* addresses critical information that reflects the national standards for coaches (NASPE, 1995) that will help coaches provide quality sport experiences in the context of a healthy social-psychological and ethical environment.

This book is designed for individuals who want to coach and make a positive impact on the character development of their players. Its purpose is to provide coaches with an understanding of the relationship between values, decision-making, and coaching behavior as they affect athletes' character development. It also provides a template for analyzing and planning how to deal with problem situations that typically may occur during a coaching season. This analysis gives coaches a guideline for examining the motives and intentions behind their actions.

The author believes that most coaches want to do more than develop the skill ability of their players. A large percentage of interscholastic and youth sport coaches have a sincere desire to make a difference in the lives of their athletes. However, in many instances this desire evolves into a need to win. Winning has become synonymous with success. Winning can be important, however, for this book to be useful, a coach must want to influence more than the attitudes of athletes toward today's game. He or she must want to influence player attitudes and behavior toward other people and to help shape the development of their values.

How the Values of Coaches Matter

This book is designed to help coaches examine their own values and consider how they influence their athletes. It asks them what lessons they want athletes to learn. While philosophy and ethics are not usually considered exciting bedtime reading, there is a need to examine the lessons that athletes learn on the playing field. This book provides a practical approach to a subject that is sometimes treated as abstract and theoretical or is reduced to rhetoric. Using common coaching problems, it explores the meaning of coaching decisions and actions and how they can influence the character development of athletes. It uses common coaching problems as a vehicle for understanding the message players receive from the decisions and actions coaches make and implement.

This book is written for coaches who work with athletes in a context that has a developmental or an educational foundation. This includes community youth and interscholastic coaches. It sometimes includes intercollegiate coaches, but it may not include professional coaches. It will have little impact or usefulness for coaches who view winning as the primary or essential goal for all sport experience.

A Hands-On Approach

The strength and uniqueness of this book lie in its applied, hands-on treatment of some very complex, theoretical areas of philosophy and ethics. It offers a user-friendly approach for people who probably would not choose to pick up a book on ethics or philosophy but who want to do the "right thing" as coaches of young people. This book elicits self-reflection. The vignettes in Part I and scenarios in Part II invite emotional reactions from the reader.

Working with preservice professionals in teacher education, the author found that the emotional responses to the scenarios are often more reliable indicators of basic beliefs and values than a theoretical discussion of "what I think my values are." Thus, the author used real-life common coaching problems as a vehicle for helping teachers and coaches better understand how their values and beliefs affect their behavior. Using emotional reactions as a starting point has been an effective pedagogical tool for analyzing and prioritizing the values that underlie an issue. Once these values are identified, choosing how to act can take on new clarity and purpose. As a result, coaches can focus on acting in ways that consistently reflect the message they want to send to their athletes.

Vignettes, Scenarios, and Team-Related Issues

The book is divided into three parts. Part I provides basic introductory material on leadership, values, reasoning processes, and decision-making. The context for the presentation of this material is sport. It is not intended to be a scholarly theoretical presentation on ethics, values, or decision-making. Rather, it presents some foundation information, definitions, and decision-making paradigms that provide a framework for discussion of coaching problems presented in Parts II and III of this book. The scenarios in Part II address coaching problems that involve individual players. Part III of the book addresses coaching problems that are team-related.

The hypothetical vignettes and scenarios presented in this text are entirely fictional and are presented for demonstration purposes only. Any individuals or circumstances that resemble actual real-life events are coincidental. Moreover, the information and options for action suggested in this book do not have any formal legal basis. It is recommended that readers seek legal counsel in their own jurisdiction before taking any action that may have legal implications.

Chapter One discusses the role of the coach as a leader who can provide athletes with the opportunity to learn about being a part of a team. It defines the team as a community and it discusses how the values and leadership style of the coach can influence the understanding of players about what it means to be a part of a community. Chapter Two asks readers to think about what they want players to learn from their sport experience. To facilitate answering such a question, some terminology is defined and readers are asked to focus on the connection between their values as a coach and actions and the messages they send to players. Chapter Three discusses how rules, expectations, and the climate created by the coach can influence the behavior and values of players. It also provides examples of linkages between desirable character traits, observable player behaviors, and rules and expectations for player behavior. Chapter Four introduces several decision-making paradigms and discusses their application for analyzing ethical dilemmas. These paradigms provide an understanding and appreciation of the nature and the inherent difficulty of the coach's role as a leader. They provide a context for categorizing and understanding what often seem to be agonizing no-win decisions.

Part II begins with Chapter Five, which presents a template for analyzing common problems that occur in coaching. Not all coaching problems involve ethical dilemmas. However, how a coach chooses to deal with typical coaching problems is generally determined by the importance attached to the values that are related to the issue. Each of the scenarios in Part II examines a common coaching situation that deals with a problem or issue involving an individual player. Analysis and discussion is presented in the context of the coach having a one-on-one meeting with the athlete. Using the template presented in Chapter Five, eight common coaching problems are discussed in terms of the communication processes useful in handling them and the values that may influence the coach's decisions on how to resolve the situation in a positive way.

Part III presents four team-related issues that can undermine a positive learning environment: (1) the use of performance-enhancing supplements, (2) parent and spectator behavior, (3) initiation rites and hazing, and (4) sexual harassment. It is hoped that the information presented on these issues will give coaches some insight into ways of guiding the behavior of players that will foster positive team relationships and experiences.

PART I

Coaching, Leadership, and Values: The Team as a Community

We teach who we are.
—*Sign at a teachers' conference (Lickona, 1991, p. 71)*

CHAPTER 1

The Coach's Job Description

Hey dad—why won't they let Uncle Harry coach our baseball team? Look at what he's done for professional baseball. We could win the conference championship with a coach like him. What does his drug problem have to do with his ability to coach, anyway? I can't believe it, but it's typical school bureaucracy. The school board needs to lighten up or Smithville High is going to throw away an unbelievable opportunity. I guess we can forget about the conference title this year. It figures the school would make a decision like this!

Defining Leadership

A leader is someone who, by example or persuasion, motivates a group of individuals to move toward a common goal. In pursuit of goals, communities often establish leaders. Groups of individuals become communities when they develop two things—shared values

and common goals. Societies are large diversified communities and within them are layers of smaller communities. Individuals in societies are members of many different smaller communities. In order for communities to function as cohesive units, leaders must foster commitment to the shared values and goals of the group.

Good leaders, at any level, recognize their role in the context of the larger community of which they are a part and can often influence other adjacent communities. Because of their visibility and status, leaders represent the identity of a group and are often emulated and idolized by group members. Because a community is defined by its shared values, leaders who do not behave in ways that reflect the community's values can threaten the stability of the group.

Because of the critical role and influence of leaders, much attention has been given to identifying the qualities that make them successful. It is probably not surprising that studies of outstanding leaders reveal many different leadership styles and personalities that have been effective and successful. John Gardner (1990), an author and leader who served under six presidents in a variety of leadership capacities, did a five-year field study of leaders of large organizations. Based on his research, Gardner identified six ways good leaders distinguish themselves (Gardner, 1990, p. 4):

- *They think long-term—beyond today's game, the day's profits or losses, the quarterly report, or the season's win-loss record.*
- *They recognize their community's relationship to the larger communities of which they are a part—school, league, city, and nation.*
- *They acknowledge and influence those outside the immediate community and often solve problems that may or may not affect their immediate community.*
- *They place heavy emphasis on intangibles such as vision, values, and motivation. They are generally very intuitive and have excellent communication skills.*
- *They have the political skill to cope with problems and conflict.*
- *They think in terms of change, adaptation, and renewal. They see community organization as a variable rather than a constant. They are adept at making organizational changes to meet the needs of the community.*

The Coach as a Leader

We will refer to the leadership qualities identified by Gardner throughout our discussions of the leadership role of coaches, but first it is important to define the job of the coach by identifying his or her role as a teacher and also a manager. As teachers, coaches must have the knowledge of their sport—its skills, strategies, and fitness needs. Because coaches are usually working with a limited amount of pre-season training time, it is critical that they use their time efficiently to develop players' skills, strategic abilities, fitness levels, and psychological preparation. Even with all the technical knowledge of the sport, a coach needs to package and plan the learning experiences to maximize players' development. This requires what is referred to in the business world as managerial skills.

The National Association for Sport and Physical Education (NASPE), has developed national standards for coaches at all levels of coaching and athletic participation. These standards are applicable to beginning-level volunteer coaches as well as highly experienced master coaches at the interscholastic, intercollegiate, and international levels. The NASPE standards include eight critical categories or domains that represent essential competencies which all coaches, regardless of coaching level, should possess. They include the knowledge of and the ability to implement developmentally appropriate coaching practices in the following areas: injuries—prevention, care, and management; risk management; growth, development, and learning; training, conditioning, and nutrition; social/psychological aspects of coaching; skills, tactics, and strategies; teaching and administration; and professional preparation and development.

Although coaches may not have the same level of experience in all of these areas, it is vital that they use educationally sound training techniques appropriate for the age, maturity, and skill level of their players. Coaches who can only replicate the training they have experienced as athletes have limited resources for the job. Although they may have been masterful at the execution of skill and strategy, this does not mean they have the education or expertise to implement developmentally appropriate training techniques for the age group they will be coaching. These teaching abilities are developed through training and coaching education.

Coaches need organizational skills to make a seasonal plan as well as to design individual practices in order to be ready for the season opener. Every practice needs to incorporate progressive training in the skill, strategy, and fitness areas. Coaches also need to balance fun and challenging practice. In addition, they need problem-solving and communication skills to manage the inevitable problems that can prevent even the best teams from performing to their potential.

The Team as a Community

Sport teams are communities. They are groups of individuals brought together by a common interest. They develop common goals. Although school classrooms may be communities, the academic environment often does not have the intense focus toward a common goal nor the need to interact with other group members to the degree that a sport team does. Thus, for many young people, being part of a team may be their first experience as a member of a diverse community. Through their team experiences, players have opportunities for unique and important social experiences. The nature of the experience is influenced by the vision and values of the coach and the way the experience is structured. Being a part of a team can promote a sense of voluntary interdependence, feelings of connection, and responsibility to others as well as to the team goals.

This was insightfully described by Swift (1991), a sport journalist and graduate of Hotchkiss Preparatory School, in his reflections about his days as a goalie on the school hockey team:

"It may be just a coincidence, but none of my teammates were expelled from school while I was at Hotchkiss. Several classmates were, but no teammates. Team members would have felt betrayed if a teammate had been caught drinking or smoking during the season, so not many of them did.

During my junior year, I was in a school play, **Inherit the Wind.** *It was directed by two seniors, who were also starring in the roles of William Jennings Bryant and Clarence Darrow. It was an enjoyable experience, and I thought of the cast as a team. You did not want to be late for rehearsals because of all those other people involved, people to whom you had become attached through sharing this common goal. You did not want to let them down.*

A few days before the play was scheduled to be performed, the two directors were caught smoking marijuana and were expelled. The play had to be canceled. I don't remember much about those two, except that neither of them played on a sports team, and I cannot help think-

ing, wrongheaded as it might be, that if they had, they would have better understood that we had entered into a sort of pact of voluntary interdependence. They would not have risked letting us down." (pp. 430-431)

The Shared Values of School Teams

As a community within a community, a sport team reflects the values both of the larger school community and of the leader. Because the identity of the school is often synonymous with the success of its sports teams, it is not uncommon for there to be external pressure to have winning seasons. The common goal for the team is often influenced by the values and needs of others, such as the school administration, the student body, parents of team members, or town citizens.

It is not unusual for coaches to be hired based on their reputations as athletes or their win-loss records. It is assumed that if they are good athletes, they can teach someone else, and that the win-loss record is the best yardstick for measuring what was taught on the sports field. It is not surprising that a capitalistic society values winning, or that worth is validated by winning. It is unfortunate, however, that it is usually not the qualities of the winner that are being honored but only the end product—winning.

Many social scientists believe that because of its emphasis on winning, competitive sport cannot positively influence character development (Orlick, 1978; Kohn, 1992). In fact, there is very little research support for the widely believed adage that competitive sports build character (Miracle & Rees, 1994; Shields & Bredemeier, 1995, 2001). However, there is evidence that indicates the coach has considerable influence on players' self-perception and psychosocial experience (Brustad, Babkes, & Smith, 2001). Given these findings, it is even more important that coaches examine the message and impact their visions, values, and behaviors have on their players.[1]

---

[1] Whether it is the role of the school to teach values is beyond the scope of discussion here. It is a subject of much debate. It is the author's belief that young people are influenced by teachers' and coaches' values, whether it is done with intention or not. With that as a given, it is important for coaches to examine the messages their actions send to the young people who play for them.

Keeping the Big Picture in the Foreground

Just as the outcome of games is determined by the one-on-one battles on playing fields, the values of a society are influenced by the shared values of the smaller communities within it. Recall three of Gardner's important qualities of good leaders: they think long-term rather than short-term; they recognize how their communities fit into the bigger picture, and they place heavy emphasis on vision, values, and motivation. Decisions made by leaders with these qualities focus on maintaining the integrity of their communities. They do this by prioritizing each community's values as ends in themselves, by taking action that is consistent with those values, and by choosing to act in ways that keep the integrity of the community in the foreground, even if it means making winning the second priority.

Having a vision means keeping the long-term best interests of the community in focus, while dealing with the short-term issues. According to Gardner's criteria, leaders who do not believe that their community values affect the bigger picture are not effective leaders. Gardner also suggests that effective leaders see beyond their immediate community. Coaches who extend their influence beyond their players to parents and fans, for example, are more likely to achieve the goals of the group. Leaders must do two things: (1) create a community, which by definition means developing shared values, and (2) motivate that community to achieve a common goal.

Life Skills: What Are We Teaching Our Children?

Without shared values, a group is not a community. Shared values are the glue that binds community members together. As leaders, effective coaches motivate community members to behave in ways that are consistent with the group's shared values. Particularly important are the values that underlie how team members treat each other. Qualities such as honesty, respect for others, fairness, cooperation, compassion, and tolerance are all prosocial constructs that provide a framework for fostering positive relationships with other people. Coaches who prioritize these qualities as important shared values see the process of being part of a team as an end in itself. They view the social context of sport as an opportunity to learn how to work with others. The shared values of the team are viewed as more important than the community's common goal. In other words, they view the team as an *intentional community*. In addition, the social experience of team members is not limited to working with others within the community. They also interact with others outside the immediate community, including officials, athletic trainers, opponents, parents, and spectators.

Sociologists generally agree that the litmus test for the health of a society is the strength of its framework of values, norms of conduct, and moral order. Healthy communities thrive because of their shared values. This was effectively noted by Gardner (1990):

> *If we look at the array of societies described by historians and anthropologists, we cannot find an instance of a healthy society in which humans have not devised a framework of values, norms of conduct, a moral order. When the community's broad consensus disintegrates or loses its force, the society sickens. People no longer find meaning in their lives. Nothing holds together. (p. 76)*

The Common Goal

It is not hard to figure out why winning is the common goal of most sport teams. It is the logical goal for a group of individuals who are engaged in a sport activity that has a built-in zero-sum outcome—a winner and a loser. There is nothing inherently wrong with wanting to win, but it gets a lot of bad press. Why? One reason may be that winning has been given priority over other values that are considered important in our society.

When rules are intentionally broken, for example, it becomes clear that the need to win has been given higher priority than honesty or fairness. Communities that don't have honesty and fairness as core values will need strict laws, an enforcement system, and strong repercussions for noncompliance. Community members no longer feel a sense of trust. Trust is believing that behavior will reflect the priority of values the group has established. If shared values are the glue that binds communities together, then mistrust can lead to community deterioration. Valuing winning is not the problem. It only becomes problematic when the desire to win displaces a core value of the community and thus threatens that community's stability and cohesiveness.

When winning is viewed as the most important purpose of sport contests, it is easy to lose sight of some of the valuable learning experiences that can occur as part of being a team member. Qualities like dedication, perseverance, responsibility, and self-control are character traits often associated with successful people. The structure of the team experience can foster the development of these qualities. However, they are not automatic by-products of the experience. Learning to be a team player and a productive community member can be both the process and the product of sport participation, but the experience needs to be designed with these outcomes in mind.

The Community Comes First

Learning to be a good community member and winning are not necessarily mutually exclusive. We often think that focusing on process outcomes means jeopardizing the win-loss record, which is the product outcome. However, if we examine the qualities of effective leaders, it becomes clear that good leaders emphasize the health of their community first and foremost. A healthy community has defined values, clear expectations for behavior and consistently applied rules and standards. A coach who focuses on the process of maintaining a healthy team environment, and who places emphasis on the intangibles of vision, values, and motivation can be successful, regardless of how the common goal is defined.

Goal orientation, perseverance, and a strong work ethic are advantageous qualities in a competitive society. Winners have these qualities. In order for a contest to have meaning, both teams must really want to win. If they don't, the contest has no purpose. This point was made effectively by Swift (1991):

> . . . Competitiveness is facing up to the fundamental truth that the purpose of the game is to win.
> . . . Pretend, for a moment, that there was such a thing as non-competitive chess. Winning or losing doesn't matter; you're in it just for the "fun." Players attack recklessly. They don't plan or anticipate or defend. They just move pieces willy-nilly about the board, no strategy,

no passion, no care. In the process they have ruined the essence of the game.

*Most people accept that argument when it is made about chess, because it is a cerebral game. But for some reason, people do not see that physical games, like tennis and baseball and soccer, are also destroyed in a fundamental way if the participants are not carefully trying to win. That does not mean that winning is the **only** thing, . . . it just means that you respect your opponent and the sport enough to try your hardest, to attempt strategy, and to exploit strengths and weakness.*

If the effort to win is missing, then none of the rest of it matters. Obeying the rules does not matter. Being a reliable teammate does not matter. Having a good coach does not matter. All these matter only if both sides are trying to win. . . . We learn something from winning and something different from losing. But what do we learn from not caring? We should care, whether it is the varsity or intramural level— or else everyone is wasting their time. (p. 429)

Teaching athletes to set goals they care about is an important lesson. Parents want their children to achieve their goals and be winners. But they also want them to be happy and live a good life. Family and community are a big part of that dream. Where do young people learn about the responsibility to the shared values of a community? The vision part of being a leader is helping the community members choose the right goals and pursue them in a way that is consistent with the values of the community.

Expectations of the School District

Although every coach has personal motives for coaching that determine how competitive he or she is, the school district's expectations for the coach and team can have tremendous influence. As a part of the larger community, school district leaders have the power to hire, fire, influence, and override the decisions of their coaches. It isn't uncommon for coaches to be told that they must have winning seasons in order to have their contracts renewed. Coaches who want to continue coaching may feel they have no choice but to adjust their behavior to reflect that desire. In this respect, the coach is middle management who often does not have final decision-making authority.

A mismatch between the coach's and the district's emphasis on winning can lead to problems. It is difficult for coaches to communicate effectively and consistently with players when their coaching values and behavior are being dictated by the district, especially if they are not comfortable with them. Just as young people receive inconsistent and mixed messages when parents disagree on issues, so do athletes who play for coaches whose actions are inconsistent because they must defer to the wishes of school administrators. Consider the following scenario:

Coach Johnson had a zero-tolerance policy toward violence. Players were encouraged to avoid situations on and off the field that had the potential to escalate into violence. His team rules stated that any player caught in a physical altercation with anyone during the season would be benched for the next game. Two violations were grounds for expulsion from the team. All players and their parents signed a copy of the team rules at the beginning of the season.

Friday night, before the game against the rival high school team, Bill, the starting quarterback, was at the local video store when he ran into a couple of players from the other school. A trash-talking dialogue escalated into a fight, and Bill was pinned against the building wall. He kicked his assailant in the shins and punched him in the face. The boy fell to the ground, letting him free. Bill jumped in his car and left. The next day, Bill was issued a warrant on assault and battery charges. The player he hit had a broken nose and jaw and had filed charges.

Hearing about the incident, Coach Johnson called Bill into his office and asked him what happened. Although Bill claimed he was not the instigator, which Coach Johnson believed was probably true, he was still in violation of the team rule. Following through with his rule, Coach Johnson told Bill he was benched for the rival game. Later that day, the athletic director informed Coach Johnson that the principal had called, saying that he wanted Bill to start in the game. The coach could bench him for another game, but not this one.

If he did not know it before, Coach Johnson now knew that his priorities and those of the district were in conflict. In this case, winning the rival game was more important to the district than following through with a clearly established team rule on violence. Thus, Coach Johnson learned rather publicly that he did not have the authority to enforce his rules when they were not in agreement with the administration. For a coach with a clear sense of values and a desire to establish consistent boundaries for player behavior, the message here is a serious one. The coach's options are limited. Some of the scenarios that follow in Part II may help you to sort out and choose among some of the options.

Questions for Consideration

So what about hiring Uncle Harry? He was an outstanding athlete and player. He certainly has knowledge of the game. But what about his leadership qualities? What shared values would he establish for his team? Would his behavior reflect the values you would like to see the team members model? Running down Gardner's leadership qualities, how would you rate him? Does he have any coaching education or training that indicates he can push the physical and emotional limits of his players safely? Would he be the type of leader that is most suitable to teach young people how to be a healthy and productive team player?

CHAPTER 2

Leadership and Character Development

You can discover more about a person in an hour of play than in a year of conversation.

—Plato

Do you remember the time that Coach Fairbanks pulled Joshua out of the Pittsfield game because he grabbed the halfback's face guard? Or the time he benched Doug, our leading scorer, because he skipped practice? We lost that game, but I don't remember too many people missing practice after that. You didn't mess with Fairbanks' rules; there were always repercussions. He never yelled, but he didn't have to, because his actions spoke louder than his words.

I remember when I was in a slump and the coach pulled me aside. He told me I needed to improve my pass completion percentage if I wanted to remain the starting quarterback. I knew he meant it, but he was nice about it. He asked me if anything was bothering me and let me know his door was open if there was something on my mind. It was a wake-up call. I appreciated it, and I worked harder after that. I wanted to keep my starting spot and didn't want to disappoint the coach.

This short reminiscence tells us a lot about Coach Fairbanks. First, he was fair. When he made rules, he enforced them uniformly. It didn't matter whether you were the leading scorer or the weakest player on the team; when it came to his rules, he was consistent and stuck to them. He based his team selection on skill. The best players played, and if you worked hard and improved, you had a chance of getting into the starting lineup. On the other hand, there were no guarantees. If you were a starter and you stopped producing, you risked losing playing time.

Second, he cared about his players. Fairbanks was there if you needed him. The door was open, and he really wanted you to succeed. If you had a problem, he would listen and help. He realized that life off the field sometimes affected how you played. He still expected 100 percent from you, but he gave it back. You were not just his athlete, you were a human being with a life.

The description of Coach Fairbanks wasn't physical; we have no idea about his lifestyle or his win-loss record. Yet, based on this short scenario, you probably have some idea whether this is a coach for whom you would like to play. In fact, the information in this description tells us about his character by describing the values that are important to him. His belief in these values serves as the motivation for his behavior and the way he leads his team.

Character

The term *character* comes from a Greek term meaning "enduring mark." Character traits are the distinguishing qualities or attributes that define an individual. The term describes the principles or beliefs that serve as the underlying motivation and guide for an individual's behavior. The behavior of people who act on principles is usually consistent and their actions are often predictable, even in situations that may have a negative personal impact.

For example, consider the following situation.

You are the girls' varsity basketball coach. Mary enrolls in the school as a new student in the district. At 6-feet 2-inches tall and only a sophomore, she is an outstanding basketball player. You have recently learned that she actually lives in the neighboring school district's legal boundaries. That district has a poor girls' basketball team, while your program is one of the strongest in the state. No one has questioned Mary's residency status.

Although it would be advantageous to play Mary, it would violate district policy and give the team an unfair competitive advantage. What would a coach who valued honesty do? If the coach decided against playing Mary out of fear of getting caught, would that be different from not playing her because it is dishonest?

Character is revealed through actions and the motives behind them. But what does the term "good character" really mean; what does it look like? Character is the composite description of an individual that identifies the personal qualities that motivate his or her behavior. Although these qualities are often abstract, when an individual consistently demonstrates those abstract qualities, we can describe that behavior as a character trait.

Consistency

Coaches who want to influence players' character development need to make decisions and behave in ways that reflect the values they want their players to learn. If honesty and fairness are important values, it would be difficult to imagine circumstances that would cause a coach to overlook evidence that would compromise those values. It would be "out of character." On the other hand, if players see that the coach is willing to overlook some rules, the players may be confused because this may not be consistent with the coach's expectations for players' behavior.

Table 1
Positive Character Qualities for Athletes

• Show respect for the game by playing by the rules, both in their spirit and their literal interpretation.

• Show responsibility by coming prepared and on time for practices and games.

• Display commitment and perseverance by giving consistent effort in practices and games.

• Accept victory with humilty and defeat with pride in the effort made.

• Show self-control and respect for others by accepting officials' calls without inappropriate comments or gestures.

• Show care for others by being supportive of teammates through comments and actions during practices and games.

• Maintain self-control and composure when things don't go in desired ways.

Traditions and expectations for behavior have been established for competitive sport participants in an effort to foster a positive learning environment and influence character development. Table 1 gives some examples of standards for behavior that reflect positive character qualities in the context of a sport setting.

There are no guarantees that sport participants will develop these character qualities or that the behaviors players demonstrate on the sports field will carry over into other areas of their lives. However, when competitive sport takes place in an educational context, the intent can be to create an environment that develops interpersonal skills. If there is a positive impact on participants' character, that would be an added benefit to the many reasons to involve young people in competitive sport.

Reinforce Behavior Through Rituals

Coaches can help players understand the reason for some of the sport rituals by explaining why they are important. For example, shaking hands after a game demonstrates respect for the opponent and the effort made in the game. Acknowledging the feelings of the losing team and accepting a win with humility are demonstrations of compassion. Helping a teammate or opponent up after a fall, whether through your fault or not, demonstrates caring and consideration. Coaches can help players understand the meaning of some sport rituals by positively reinforcing such behaviors. This can be done at the moment, such as right after a player has helped someone up that the player unintentionally fouled, and then followed up later by mentioning the good example of self-control and consideration of others during the game. Players are quick to recognize what behaviors coaches look for. The coach's body language and comments are strong cues to players about what is important. Referencing the connection between the behavior and underlying value it represents reinforces the community bond of the team.

Another way a coach might reinforce and make connections between rituals and behavior is during team meetings. Talking about positive and negative events that occurred in the league or in professional sports is a good way to generate discussion about rituals and their purpose. Discussions about players who refuse to shake hands with opposing team members at the end of a game, for example, is a good way to help players make the connection between the behavior and self-control, anger management, and how to keep the game in perspective, as well as respect for the skill, hard work, and accomplishments of others.

Personal and Team Goals

Good character also involves the commitment, perseverance, and resilience to work toward goals for the benefit of the team as well as personal gain. It means taking responsibility to follow through on commitments to others, including the larger community players represent—teammates, opponents, coaches, officials, and fans. To the best of a player's ability, this means following the team and school rules as well as the laws of the community at large. It means believing in and behaving in ways that are consistent with the shared values of the team and larger community of which it is a part.

Although a team's goal may be to have a winning season, the common goal can also be defined in terms of performance excellence and improvement. It may not be surprising that coaches who view performance excellence, improvement, and effort as primary team goals often find they do well in the win-loss column, too. Moreover, it is difficult to improve or achieve excellence without dedication, hard work, and perseverance. If these qualities are among a team's shared values, a coach who is focused on maintaining the health of the community is also working to achieve the team's common goal. More discussion of the definition of team success, winning, and performance excellence will be discussed in Chapter 3.

Values [1]

Values serve as guides for behavior and decision-making. A value is something that is seen as having relative worth. It is a

---

[1]According to an extensive literature review by Timms (1983), there are over 180 definitions of the term "value." At the risk of oversimplification, a working definition is presented here to provide the reader with an understanding of the construct in order to work through the scenarios in Part II of the book. A more extensive discussion of the term "value" can be found in *Character Development and Physical Activity* (Shields & Bredemeier, 1995) and *Educating for Character: How Our Schools Can Teach Respect and Responsibility* (Lickona, 1991).

culturally derived personal preference. We can value something tangible, like material possessions, or something abstract, like honesty. Winning, skill, fame, and money are all examples of things that may be valued, as are dedication, persistence, and loyalty.

The description of Coach Fairbanks by his players provides insight into his character and the principles that guided his actions. If winning were the only thing that was important, he would not have benched his leading scorer for missing practice. By doing so, Fairbanks let his players know that he valued responsibility to the team more than winning the game. He created a community

environment based on his beliefs about what was important. His values provided the framework for his players' experiences under his leadership.

Coaches' values have tremendous influence on their players. In fact, players are often more aware of what the coach values than the coach is. Consider what the players remembered about Coach Fairbanks.

They remembered his character—traits such as caring, fairness, and responsibility. What do these traits have in common? They all deal with how he treated other people. How a leader treats other people is important for two reasons. First, it serves as a role model for the behavior of the team members. Second, it defines and reflects the shared values of the community, which can lead to a more stable and cohesive team.

But modeling behavior that reflects community values is only part of a coach's influence on players' character development. Effective leadership in teaching situations also needs to address the reasoning processes that underlie decisions. Players who understand the reasoning process and the motives behind them are better equipped to make decisions based on their values. In the example regarding residency, if the coach chose not to play Mary out of fear of getting caught, and not because it violated his or her fundamental principles, the result would be the same. However, the two motives provide insight into very different character descriptions.

Leadership Style

As the team leader, the coach is the catalyst for the development of the goals and shared values that will ultimately define the community. Consider the contrasting leadership styles of the two coaches described below:

> *Coach Fox was a taskmaster. Everyone worked hard during her practice. Each drill was timed to the second. I remember kids actually throwing up after the final wind sprints. And if you were last in the sprints, you risked being given laps to run before you left practice. Everybody feared Coach Fox. But she got the job done, and the team was always prepared on game day.*
>
> *Funny thing was, though, when Coach Fox wasn't verbally pushing us, kids really slacked off. I remember once she sent us around the school for a final lap. Well, a couple of people cut through the school and led the pack coming around the final corner. No one said anything to the coach, but there were some really angry people. The coach really had to push us when she was there, because no one worked hard when she wasn't.*

> *Coach Ramirez worked us hard and was very organized, but he involved the team in the process of making the rules and setting the goals. At the time, I think we might have thought of him as a pushover, but looking back on it, I realize that we probably pushed ourselves because we felt we owned a piece of the dreams and goals. We were a unit, and it was important to him that we took part in the decision-making process. It was also important to him that we thought about the reasons for what we were doing.*
>
> *I remember that Coach Ramirez had a meeting with every single team member and asked what our personal goals were. For those of us with big dreams, he helped you figure out a way to get there. And if you had the dream, but weren't willing to do what it took to get there—well, the meeting was a reality check. I remember Tommy Schwartz wanted a college scholarship. Coach set him up with an off-season training program that he could do on his own. And Tommy did it—all summer long!*

Coaches' leadership styles reflect their goals and values as well as their communication skills and the amount of decision-making freedom they give to their players. Often more important than what is said is the manner in which the message is delivered. Some coaches encourage athletes to be a part of the decision-making process and to think independently while others encourage uniformity, compliance, and loyalty. Some coaches command respect through fear, intimidation, and shame, while others work to develop pride and commitment through self-discipline, clearly defined personal goals, and improved performance. As noted in the contrasting descriptions of Coaches Fox and Ramirez, when players take part in the decision-making and goal-setting process, they are more likely to be self-motivated to achieve their goals. This can result in greater progress and improvement because they are more likely to work hard without someone monitoring them every step of the way. In addition, coaches who treat players with respect are more likely to develop the players' sense of self-respect as well as respect for the coach.

The Decision-Making Process

But what about character development? What style of leadership best develops good character? Role models play a strong part in character development. However, doing the right thing is only the end product. The reasoning process that leads to the decision is also important. Hence, a leadership style that does not provide opportunities for players to make decisions will probably have limited impact on the connections players make between actions and the reasons for them.

As will become more clear in Chapter 4, values and beliefs serve as the foundation for decisions. In order for team members to understand the connection between beliefs, values, and the resulting decisions, three things are necessary. First, they must identify the values and beliefs that are important to the team. Second, they need to understand what types of actions demonstrate their beliefs. Third, they must be given opportunities to take part in reasoning and decision-making processes that involve values important to the team.

Team discussions that involve identifying and prioritizing values help players learn how to make decisions. They also expose players to other points of view and different reasoning processes. Further, they are opportunities to develop communication skills. In discussing past decisions, players gain insight into the factors considered and have an opportunity to express their feelings and thoughts about the issues involved. Leaders who take the opportunity to involve players in making decisions, and who listen to their thoughts and feelings, demonstrate respect for their players and strengthen the commitment to team goals and shared values.

Young people on sport teams have an opportunity to participate in a community with a set of common values that frame their experiences. As leaders, coaches can influence their players' attitudes, beliefs, and behaviors in all aspects of sports. This includes teammates, opponents, the game itself, the rules, authority figures, the arena of competition, winning and losing, work ethic, and self-esteem.

Team Captains

Another way coaches influence players is the way they delegate leadership. There are a number of ways to select team captains, and the choice is partly determined by how the coach defines the job. The strengths and limitations of the players on the team are also factors that will affect the choice.

Team captains should have good listening skills, be approachable by all players, and be able to say things tactfully. They need to be able to make independent decisions, have a strong work ethic, dedication to the team, a conscience, be honest, compassionate, and fair. Just as the coach has to behave in ways that reflect the team values, so do the captains. Because they are role models for their teammates, captains should represent the qualities the coach wants other players to emulate. The rules in some team sports require that there is a player designated as captain in the game at all times. This player has specific game-related responsibilities such as addressing the official or calling time outs. In these sports, coaches need to have a plan for meeting this rule. This is particularly true when the most-skilled players do not have the personal qualities to be effective team leaders.

Coaches make evaluative judgments about players on a daily basis. There is not always time to give players the one-on-one attention they need. Unexplained decisions can result in communication problems or player misperceptions. For this reason, one vital role of team captains is keeping the communication lines open between players and the coach. Sometimes they need to decide what the coach needs to hear or not hear.

Picking a Captain

Depending on what role the coach wants the captain to play, the team should have a discussion of the desired qualities for the position. This is particularly important if players will be involved in the selection. Otherwise, the process can turn into a popularity contest or power play. It can also be weighted too heavily on seniority or skill.

There is no "right way" to select a team captain. However, some methods allow for more player participation in the process. Several common methods are listed below.

- The coach designates the number of captains and makes the selection.
- Two captains are selected. The coach chooses one, the team votes on one.
- Captains rotate each week. Selection is based on specified criteria evaluated during practices. Coach or players make the selection.
- No one is designated as the team captain. A leader is appointed for each game to do official game duties, if necessary for the sport.

There is no best method for selecting captains. The method of selection may depend on the job description and whether there are players on the team who can fulfill the role. Some coaches change their method of selection based on the needs of the team and the strengths and limitations of the players. Rotating captains allows everyone to have a chance to develop leadership skills, but lacks continuity. However, involving players in the decision-making process will provide an opportunity to discuss the qualities of a good leader.

Regardless of the method of selection, choosing leaders is a vital process in our society, and the selection of team captains can be a valuable learning experience. As will be apparent in some of the scenarios in Part II, team leaders can have a significant influence on the team as a community and can play an instrumental role in making the environment safe and positive.

How Will Your Players Describe You?

Most sport social scientists would agree that there are two methods of influencing players' character development (Weiss, 1987; Shields & Bredemeier, 1995, 2001; Stoll, Beller, & Lumpkin, 2002). One important way is having discussions among coaches and players and examining reasons for decisions. Another major source of influence is the modeling effect of the coach. Asking yourself how you want to be remembered by your players is a way to identify what is important to you as a coach. Players will be influenced by what you think is important, whether you intend this or not. Without introspection and sometimes painful self-honesty, it is often difficult to identify how we would be described by our players.

Because character is a complex trait, it may be useful to think about how you would like to influence your players. In other words, ask yourself these questions: "What qualities would I like my players to learn under my leadership? What qualities would make them better people and community members in the future?" As a follow-up to these questions, you should consider how the leadership and the community environment you have created encourages the development of these qualities. What specific things do you do to promote the development of these qualities in your players?

Identifying Your Values: Take the Challenge

Table 2 lists some of the qualities and character traits that are valued in our society. From this list, pick out the ones that you consider most important. If there are any descriptors missing from this list that you consider important, you should add them. In other words, if your players were to describe you in 25 words or less, what five or six qualities would they choose? Once you have identified those you consider most important, make a secondary list. This list will identify things that may not be as important in a sport context or just not as high a priority as those descriptors on the core list.

Using the list you generated, and looking at the image you have created, write or record what you think your players would say about you in 10 years if they were reminiscing about their playing experiences. Then ask a friend—who knows you and has seen you work with your team (and who will be honest)—to read your description. Is your self-perception accurate in the eyes of others? If it isn't, try to identify why not. If you want to impact players in the way you described, figure out what you have to do differently to be remembered that way. Once you have what you think is an accurate value statement, the next step is figuring out how to create an environment that will encourage the development of those qualities in your players. This step will be addressed in the next chapter.

Table 2
Qualities and Character Traits

Trust	Dedication	Responsiblity
Compassion	Lose with dignity	Self-control
Caring	Self-esteem	Communicate effectively
Loyalty	Perseverance	Be a good role model
Fairness	Resilience	Sportpersonship
Cooperation	Humility	Moral courage
Dignity	Strong work ethic	Commitment
Respect	Self-respect	Tactfulness
Honesty	Empathy	Win graciously
	Integrity	Set realistic goals

CHAPTER 3

Creating a Positive Environment for Character Development

Tell me and I forget, teach me and I remember, involve me and I learn.

—Benjamin Franklin

Creating a Positive Environment

Keeping in mind the role of sports in the lives of young people will help a coach create a positive environment. Most young people choose to play sports because it is fun. And it is not surprising that the most common reason young people stop playing sports is because it is no longer fun. Also, most people like doing what they are good at. However, developing skill at anything takes practice, dedication, and hard work, so the challenge for the coach is to help players develop their skills in an environment that is positive and fun.

In Chapter 1, we defined a community as a group of people with a common goal and shared values. To create a positive community environment, the coach needs to guide and shape the development of team values and goals. Coaches bring their own vision, values, and goals to their team as its leader. If a coach wants to promote personal qualities and values such as responsibility, compassion, self-discipline, commitment, and honesty, he or she needs to provide learning opportunities that foster their development.

Start Off Right

A team meeting at the beginning of the season is a good time to set the tone, to open communication between the players and coach, and to create a positive team climate. At this meeting, goals for the season and administrative details can be discussed. In addition, the group can talk about the team identity—"who we are and what we stand for."

This discussion easily segues to a discussion of what the team needs to do to accomplish its goals. For example, if one of the goals is to play a tight person-to-person defense, asking the team what they will need to do to accomplish this goal is a good way to give players input into the decision-making process. Having the players discuss what kind of attendance at practice is needed and what kind of commitment to conditioning is necessary to achieve these goals is a good way to start the season. When players are involved in figuring out what it will take to accomplish the team goals, they are empowered. When players help create rules and expectations, and understand why they are necessary, players are more positive about the rules.

Young people can work with a wide variety of leadership styles and instructional methods. They are generally flexible and adaptable. What is essential for maximizing players' growth on a physical, as well as an emotional, level is trust. Healthy communities have relationships that are built on respect, dignity, fairness, compassion, and trust. Treating players with dignity, respect, and fairness creates a foundation for developing trust. Regardless of the coach's personality or leadership style, these values are the foundation of a healthy team and create a climate for character-building educational experiences.

Creating a Caring Environment

A longitudinal study (McNeely, Nonnemaker,& Blum, 2002) of 72,000 students in grades 7–12 found that students' sense of connectedness to school and feeling of general well-being was higher in well-managed classrooms with caring teachers. They found that class climate improves and participation in high-risk health behaviors decreases when teachers are empathetic, consistent, encourage student self-management, and involve students in the decision-making process.

Neither class size nor type of school—public, private, urban, or suburban—was as important a factor as the caring environment teachers create. These findings corroborate earlier studies that identified caring as a characteristic of effective teachers (Bosworth, 1995; Gubacs, 1997; Wentzel, 1997). Goodman, Sutton, and Harkavy (1995) suggest that teachers who care enhance social growth as well as achievement. They found that a caring climate promotes personal learning and performance excellence regardless of teachers' choice of instructional methodology.

These findings suggest that coaches who genuinely care about their players may positively impact their performance and result in fewer behavioral problems. Players may be more likely to self-monitor and comply with the expectations and rules of the team if they believe that the coach cares about them as individuals. Demonstrating to players that you care about them takes time. Although you can tell them, actions speak louder than words. Players will draw their own conclusions as the coach interacts with them over the course of the season.

Expectations

Expectations are behaviors the coach wants to promote but cannot monitor on a consistent and ongoing basis. For example, a coach may expect players to keep themselves in good shape mentally and physically during the season. It is reasonable to expect players to eat well, hydrate themselves, and stay well-rested for practices and games. However, it is not reasonable for a coach to monitor every player's personal habits all season long. It is important that coaches establish and effectively communicate expectations to players. Creating expectations for players encourages them to develop personal responsibility for their behaviors. Expectations are often difficult to monitor directly. Coaches can promote behavior consistent with expectations by linking it with effort, improvement, and performance mastery whenever possible. Encouraging players to identify why they are unhappy or frustrated with their performance and to develop a plan for progress is a way of helping students self-monitor and develop behaviors that are consistent with expectations. Individual goal-setting meetings with players can be a good time to help players on an individual basis.

Rules

Rules are boundaries that define appropriate and inappropriate behavior. If everyone in a community prioritized the same values and acted consistently in accordance with those values, there would be no need for rules. Rules in communities, like laws in society, are needed because the same values and internal moral compasses do not always serve as the foundation for everyone's behavior.

Rules are most effective when they define specific behaviors that the coach can directly observe. Rules that cannot be enforced will not be perceived as effective. Examples of effective rules are:

- Players will exhibit verbal and nonverbal behavior that demonstrates self-control and respect for others.
- Players must attend the practice before a game in order to play.
- Players must be in school on game day at the start of the school day in order to play in the game.
- Players must maintain a minimum of a 2.0 quarterly grade point average in order to be eligible for interscholastic team participation.

Setting Goals

Distinguishing between rules and expectations is important, because rules are enforceable and provide definitive boundaries for behavior. They also can have established consequences. Expectations, on the other hand, can be established by the team and the coach, which creates a sense of community and mutual responsibility. This is important because character traits and qualities such as responsibility, dedication, and self-control require self-monitoring. Players are more likely to self-monitor if they are part of the process of setting team and personal goals and creating a plan to accomplish them.

Regardless of how many years a coach has used the same team rules, it is the *process* of establishing the goals, values, and rules of the team that is important. This forms the foundation of the team as a community and sets up the learning environment. In reality, the goals, values, expectations, and rules that the team adopts may not substantially differ from year to year. However, when players are involved in the process of their adoption, their attitude toward them is significantly different. Short-cutting this process because the end result is the same misses the point.

The Decision-Making Process

If playing on a team is going to impact athletes' character development, they need to be a part of the decision-making process. What is the purpose of the process? First, it establishes that the coach respects the players and gives them a voice in the decisions that are made. Second, it provides opportunities for the players to initiate discussion of the reasons for the expectations and rules; it begins the process of associating values with behaviors that exemplify them. Third, it gives players a voice in identifying the consequences or repercussions for rule noncompliance. Fourth, it establishes the team climate during the discussion and adoption process, and the players get to know the coach.

Once the team has established goals, expectations, and rules, it is a good idea to put them in writing and have the players bring them home for their parents to sign. This is particularly helpful when players' compliance with the rules is dependent on parental responsibility as well, such as getting to practice on time. As will be discussed in Part III, holding a meeting with parents can be an effective preventive measure for problems that often arise during the season.

Consequences for Breaking the Rules

There is a large body of literature on the subject of discipline, and there are many different approaches and philosophies regarding its use. Presentation of these varied approaches is beyond the scope of discussion here, except to suggest that the coach who wants to develop the self-control, responsibility, and self-esteem of players needs to develop a discipline plan that is consistent with the development of these qualities.

To build self-esteem, players need to be treated with dignity. This means using private rather than public discussion of misbehavior. The discussion should be done with a quiet but firm tone and is more effective if the coach is in proximity to the athlete at the time of delivery. Although imparting consequences for misbehavior may not seem like an esteem-building event, using a procedure that preserves the dignity of the players is conducive to its development.

Responsibility

Coaches whose primary focus is obedience, who have a "my way or the highway" mentality, may promote neither dignity nor responsibility in their players. The obedience model may not promote self-control because players' behavior is controlled by someone else externally. Developing responsibility and self-control in players requires a balance of power between the coach and players. It also requires giving time to the learning process. Players need to have opportunities to make choices and mistakes. In order to develop self-control, players need to be involved in the decision-making process about the rules as well as in the choices about their behavior. Giving players opportunities to make decisions and using natural consequences to teach them about their mistakes can be time consuming. A coach whose priority is to win may be more comfortable with an obedience model because it may seem like a more efficient use of time.

Applying Rules Fairly

Rules are most effective when there are consequences for noncompliance. In general, establishing clear consequences when the rule is made promotes fairness and consistency. Of course, it also limits coaches' options. If there are circumstances that would lead the coach not to apply the same consequences in virtually all situations, then it would be better not to specify them. When consequences are not applied consistently, players begin to question the coach's fairness.

As long as the rules and consequences are clear, players will usually accept them. Inconsistent rule application by the coach is more damaging than not making a rule at all. It leads to mistrust. Players need a safe and trusting environment in order to have a positive educational sport experience. Coaches who find themselves unwilling to follow through with consequences because of the risk of losing games should ask themselves why they are coaching. Is it for the athletes' benefit or for their own need to win?

Teaching Values

Unlike physical skills, values are not directly observable. Our values are often inferred from our actions. Because children are strong visual learners, they often mimic and model the behaviors they see. Just watching how children often idolize and mimic professional athletes is evidence of the modeling effect. Modeling accounts for some of the behavior of athletes, but how much influence does it have on their actual character development?

Can character development be taught, and if so, how? There are no definitive answers to this question. However, it is generally accepted that social context plays a significant role in shaping character (Shields & Bredemeier, 2001; Sherif, 1977). Coaches are considered a significant influence in the competitive sport environment. The environment they create and their behavior as role models are key elements in the lessons that are transmitted.

There are several ways coaches can influence players' character development. One is by modeling the behavior expected of the players. Another is establishing and maintaining clear and consistent boundaries for players' behavior. A third is to use teachable moments as they occur in practices or games and to make time for discussions about them.

Using Teachable Moments

The ref probably made a bad call. Our player was given her fourth personal foul. It didn't look like Ashley had tripped her opponent, but she really mouthed off to the referee. She started swearing and slammed the ball to the floor as hard as she could. Then Ashley turned to our coach for support. She seemed sure Coach Miller had seen the injustice and would be angry, too.

Coach Miller watched Ashley's out-of-control behavior and heard her yelling at the referee. Then the coach turned to the referee and argued the call, too. I remember hearing Coach Miller say she thought the referee needed her eyes examined!

This was a teachable moment. By allowing Ashley to challenge the call on the court in anger, the coach endorsed her player's lack of self-control and disrespect for the referee. The fact that the coach also challenged the referee's call and made a disparaging comment about her eyesight demonstrated her own disrespect. The lesson taught to the players was evident. Opportunities like this occur at nearly every practice and game. The coach who wants to maximize her influence on players' behavior has two primary responsibilities. First, the desired behaviors must be demonstrated by the coach. Second, the players must be held accountable for their behaviors, especially when it is inappropriate.

Creating boundaries for behavior is an important part of the teaching and learning process. It involves making clear rules and expectations, as well as consequences for inappropriate behavior. Unlike drills for practicing physical skills, the lessons for learning in the affective domain occur when situations come up that challenge the boundaries for behavior or require a difficult decision about how to act. Quite often these situations seem to arise at the most inopportune times, and the temptation may be to overlook them. However, situations like these can become the defining moments of a coach's influence.

Connecting Values and Behavior

Coaches can capitalize on teachable moments by taking the time to discuss current events that deal with values. For example, discussing a news item about a player thrown out of a game for fighting is a good way to talk about respect for others. The discussion should be geared to the developmental level of the players, but at any level, the coach can make connections between a person's values and his or her behavior choices. Using third-party examples is also a good idea because it de-personalizes issues, allowing for more candid discussion. Discussing issues gives the coach an opportunity to hear the players' thoughts, feelings, and perceptions about situations. Discussions also allow the coach to make the connection between behavior and the character trait it represents.

Fun, Winning, and Character Development— Can You Have It All?

Is it possible to create a team environment that is fun, competitive, and positively influences character development? Or are these goals mutually exclusive? Most sport contests are zero sum, meaning that there will be a winner and a loser. If the only thing that matters is winning, then fun, winning, and character development probably are mutually exclusive. However, it is possible for the coach to establish team and individual goals for games that are more important than the final score. With realistic goals, players can  be successful, feel a sense of accomplishment, and have fun.

The coach has the power and influence to define how important winning is to the team. If the coach narrowly defines success as the win-loss record, chances are good that the team will also view it that way. When the only thing that matters is winning, it is often difficult to positively impact other aspects of the experience.

Behaviors such as cheating and aggression are more likely to occur when the need to win is the most important outcome (Kohn, 1992; Lumpkin, Stoll, & Beller, 2003). However, if other goals are incorporated, such as becoming a more skillful player or making an effective execution of a particular strategy, players can feel good about their performance (individually and collectively). They can have fun, even if they don't win.

It is possible to want to win, to have fun, and to have a positive influence on players' character development. But it does mean establishing and maintaining priorities, and it will require self-control. Like beauty, success is in the eye of the beholder. Wanting to win is not a problem. It only becomes a problem when other values such as fairness or honesty are sacrificed to attain it. Our society is a competitive one, and sport provides an opportunity for young people to learn how to be a part of a competitive community. Sport participation can be a valuable life lesson. The question is, what do we want our children to learn?

Helping Athletes Make Connections

Coaches shape the social context of athletes' experiences. They are responsible for creating the climate of the community. Coaches' expectations of players can affect how they relate to others, how they perceive themselves, and the personal qualities they develop as team members. Because some values and desirable personal qualities are not directly observable, it is helpful if players understand what type of behavior exemplifies a value or personal quality.

Table 3 demonstrates how the environment might be structured to promote the development of some of the values and positive qualities often attributed to sport participation. It also defines some personal qualities and behavioral values. For example, self-discipline is a positive personal quality that is often associated with dedicated and successful athletes. Players with self-discipline have clearly defined, realistic goals and work consistently to attain them. Their commitment is demonstrated by a high degree of focused, physical effort. This effort is made consistently, whether or not they are monitored. Players who are self-disciplined will practice and work on their own and do not need supervision or external motivation. Self-disciplined athletes comply with rules because they recognize the reasons for them rather than out of fear of negative consequences for noncompliance.

Table 3 is not intended to represent all the traits or values that can be developed through sport participation. Rather, it is intended to provide examples of how some qualities and traits can be defined in observable terms. It also demonstrates how expectations and rules can be used to foster behavior that exemplifies some of the desired traits. It is important to note that the dedication, trust, and honesty traits have limited data in the "rule" column. These traits are not easily developed or monitored with rules. Their development is more likely to be promoted and fostered with expectations that identify the team's shared values. Rules, however, are important because they outline definitive boundaries for player behavior.

Table 3

Connections Between Character Traits, Observable Behavior, Expectations, and Rules

Trait or Quality	Observable Behavior	Expectation	Rule
Responsibility	• Arrives on time for practices, games, meetings, etc. • Comes prepared with uniform and equipment. • Attends classes & hands in assignments on time. • Takes initiative to ask for help if having academic difficulty. • Displays behavior and performance that indicate physical and mental preparation for practices and games. • Completes all assigned tasks on time consistently. • Takes initiative to help others with tasks when needed.	• Works hard to reach academic potential. • Arrives on time for school and attends regularly. • Maintains health by eating, hydrating, & being well rested. • Helps teammates maintain health and eligibility and good standing in school community. • Informs coach of any issues that affect the team.	• Must maintain academic average to be eligible for team participation. • Must be in good standing in the school and larger community to be eligible for team participation. • Must be in school at the start of the school day in order to participate in games and practices. • Must be on time and prepared for all team functions.
Honesty	• Is truthful and forthright in word and action. • Follows rules and expectations of the team, school, and community at large. • Communicates with tact, respect, and truthfulness. • Admits when a team rule or expectation has not been met. • Accepts responsibility for mistakes.	• Follows team rules and expectations. • Communicates truthfully with others. • Displays behavior that is consistent with the spirit, as well as the literal interpretation, of rules. • Internalizes the values of the team and acts in ways that are consistent with them.	• Must display behavior that is consistent with the rules of the team and school, and laws of the community at large. • Must be truthful.

Table 3
Connections Between Character Traits, Observable Behavior, Expectations, and Rules

Trait or Quality	Observable Behavior	Expectation	Rule
Compassion	• Demonstrates behavior that shows regard for others' feelings. • Is tactful in word and action. • Shows remorse for actions or words that have been hurtful. • Does not intentionally hurt others physically or emotionally.	• Works hard not to verbally or physically hurt others. • Apologizes and makes amends for harm caused. • Takes initiative to help others. • Treats others as he or she would like to be treated. • Is tactful and respectful of the feelings of others.	• Must not intentionally cause physical or emotional harm to others. • Must behave in ways that are supportive and helpful to others.
Trust	• Demonstrates follow-through on verbal commitments consistently. • Follows rules consistently even when not closely monitored. • Demonstrates commitment to team rules and expectations. • Demonstrates consistency between words and actions.	• Follows all rules and expectations. • Chooses to behave in ways that are in the best interest of the team. • Is truthful. • Exercises good judgement and uses common sense.	• Must follow team rules.

Table 3
Connections Between Character Traits, Observable Behavior, Expecations, and Rules

Trait or Quality	Observable Behavior	Expectation	Rule
Self-Discipline	• Sets realistic personal goals and works consistently toward them. • Demonstrates high physical effort even when not closely monitored. • Maintains fitness level for optimal performance. • Takes advantage of opportunities for self-improvement.	• Chooses option, when given choices, that will optimize personal and team growth. • Sets and works toward individual and team goals. • Internalizes the values of the team and acts in ways that are consistent with them.	• Must follow team training programs and meet long-term standards for performance set by the coach.
Perseverance	• Applies consistent effort and works toward goals under all conditions. • Uses constructive criticism as feedback to aid improvement. • Maintains positive attitude and outlook even when things are not going well. • Sets realistic goals and works toward them consistently.	• Sets and works consistently toward team and individual goals. • Uses feedback for self-improvement. • Works through difficult times with tenacity.	• Must follow rules and training programs established for the team.

Table 3
Connections Between Character Traits, Observable Behavior, Expectations, and Rules

Trait or Quality	Observable Behavior	Expectation	Rule
Dedication	• Follows team rules and meets expectations consistently. • Exerts physical effort during all team activities consistently. • Attends all regularly scheduled practices and team events. • Comes to team events on time and prepared. • Maintains eligibility. • Puts team needs ahead of personal playing goals when appropriate.	• Helps other to achieve their personal goals. • Follows team rules consistently. • Behaves in ways that are consistent with the team values and goals.	• Must follow team rules. • Must meet eligibility standards for sport participation.
Self-Control	• Refrains from arguing or gesturing at others while playing under pressure. • Maintains neutral overt behavior even when provoked or under pressure. • Accepts criticism from authority with a neutral attitude. • Shows overt respect for others' feelings and physical safety.	• Does not intentionally harm others. • Does not challenge coaches' directives in a disrespectful way. • Uses verbal and body language that shows respect for others. • Respects traditions of the game.	• Must participate in game and team traditions such as shaking hands with opponents after contests. • Must refrain from using inappropriate language. • Must not receive technical fouls or reprimands for disrespectful behavior during games or practices.

Table 3
Connections Between Character Traits, Observable Behavior, Expecations, and Rules

Trait or Quality	Observable Behavior	Expectation	Rule
Teamwork	• Is verbally supportive of others regardless of personal stakes. • Helps others to improve. • Accepts suggestions and assignments willingly from coaches, trainers, and officials. • Sacrifices personal needs for the good of the team. • Works cooperatively with others regardless of personal differences. • Maintains positive attitude when taken out of games.	• Puts personal differences aside and works cooperatively toward common team goals. • Sacrifices personal needs for the best interests of the team. • Respects the feelings and needs of others. • Supports other team members. • Demonstrates care and concern for the needs and safety of others.	• Must be verbally and physically supportive of others on and off the field. • Must interact with others in a manner that shows respect and self-control.
Respect for Teammates	• Treats all team members with dignity and respect even when there may be negative feelings. • Keeps comments about other team members positive. • Resolves interpersonal conflicts with teammates through direct discussion or through mediation. • Refrains from comments or body language that demonstrate contempt or disapproval of other players.	• Is supportive of teammates on and off the field. • Resolves conflicts directly in nonconfrontational ways or uses a responsible mediator. • Prioritizes the needs of the team above personal preferences. • Keeps opinions about others to self.	• Must refrain from derogatory public comments or talk about others. • Must accept differences of others. • Must refrain from physically or emotionally harming others. • Must use appropriate verbal and body language when communicating with others.

CHAPTER 4

Decision-Making and Values

Tell me to what you pay attention and I will tell you who you are.

—Jose Ortega y Gasset

Leadership and Decision-Making

Tough decisions are inevitable. No matter how introspective and evolved a person you think you are, some decisions will always be difficult and heart-wrenching. This doesn't mean that you are indecisive, or that you lack the strength to take a stand. Ironically, those who have the hardest time making difficult decisions are usually the people who are most in touch with their values. They care about the consistency of their values, their actions, and the impact they have on others.

Coaches, as leaders and teachers, have substantial influence and control over their athletes. They are responsible for structuring the environment and the learning experiences of their athletes. If young people are to learn to make decisions based on principles, they need to have experiences that exemplify that type of decision-making. They also need to understand reasoning processes and have opportunities to take part in decision-making. In order to help players in their development, coaches need to be in touch with their own decision-making and reasoning processes.

Passing the Baton: Teaching About Decision-Making

Just as the aggregate number of individual battles on the playing field determines the outcome of games, the composite of the coach's decisions and actions determines what values players learn. Although unstructured sport activities can be meaningful learning experiences, one difference between a recreational activity and an educational one is the intent of the leader. Research findings on competitive sport participation and positive character development are not encouraging (Kohn, 1992; Miracle & Rees, 1994; Orlick, 1978; Shields & Bredemeier, 2001). However, that does not mean that learning has not occurred (Brustad, Babkes, & Smith, 2001). The question is, what has been taught? The influence of coaches and the social context of the sport environment have an impact on players' experience. If we want sport experiences to have a positive influence on character development, we need to coach with that intent in mind.

In our society, winning is extremely important. That message appears to be clearly received by athletes. It probably would not surprise us to find that most people believe "it isn't how you play the game, it's whether you win or lose." Coaches who focus on the importance of effort, improvement, and performance excellence, rather than winning, may be more likely to have a positive impact on character development.

Scholastic and youth sport experiences have the potential to be effective environments for developing positive character traits. Coaches who want to influence character development must first commit to that goal. Coaches also need to examine their decisions and identify the underlying values that motivated their actions. This reflective process works like a mirror. When coaches step back and look at the message their actions give, they better understand how they are perceived by their athletes.

For a coach who wants to promote positive character development, a team is an intentional community, one that is designed to focus first on the process of creating shared values and second on the common goal. For example, coaches who prioritize winning over values such as playing by the rules or respecting others are not promoting character development. If character development is the intent, winning cannot take priority over the shared values of the team as a community.

Solving Moral Dilemmas

Coaches who care about their messages will find that working through the dilemmas presented in this chapter will help identify their values and their reasoning processes. There is an entire field of ethics that deals with solving dilemmas that involve competing values. It is grounded in the works of ancient philosophers and can be difficult to understand without a background in philosophy. However, philosopher Rushworth Kidder (1995) has written a book—*How Good People Make Tough Choices: Resolving the Dilemmas of Ethical Living*—that presents this information in a framework that can be easily understood and applied.

Kidder constructed a paradigm for decision-making that categorizes types of decisions. In particular, his paradigm involves decisions that juxtapose two moral values, creating a "no wrong answer" or "right-versus-right" dilemma. Moral values are abstract virtuous behaviors that are subjective and internal. They are derived from feelings, thoughts, deduction, or intuition and are influenced by social, cultural, and historical norms and contexts. Because they are internal, moral values cannot be seen directly and thus are often inferred from behavior. Honesty, responsibility, fairness, cooperation, caring, and respect are examples of moral values. Usually when the term "character" is used, it refers to virtuous qualities that are based on moral values. Recall the description of Coach Fairbanks in Chapter 3. What his athletes most remembered were his sense of trust, his fairness, and how he cared about his players.

There are many types of values other than moral ones. Categories of nonmoral values are cultural, political, material, educational, religious, and economic (Shields & Bredemeir, 1995).[1] It is important to point out that there is nothing wrong with placing importance on nonmoral values. It is legitimate to value education, money, winning, and material possessions such as a car. Their importance only becomes problematic when a nonmoral value, such as money, is given priority over a moral value, such as honesty.

---

[1] The purpose of the discussion of moral and nonmoral values here is to provide basic definitions for the reader to use in working through the decision-making dilemmas presented in Part II of the book. Interested readers may find a more in-depth presentation of these concepts in *Character Development and Physical Activity* (Shields & Bredemeier, 1995).

Human relationships, whether they involve two people or a whole community, rely heavily on moral values for their foundation. Kidder's Moral Decision-Making Paradigm examines dilemmas that pit two moral values against each other. In order to make a decision, one moral value must be given priority. These types of decisions are often the most difficult to make and are "defining moments" because they reveal much about an individual's character.

Kidder's Moral Decision-Making Paradigm[2]

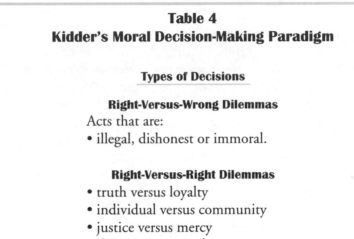

Table 4
Kidder's Moral Decision-Making Paradigm

Types of Decisions

Right-Versus-Wrong Dilemmas
Acts that are:
• illegal, dishonest or immoral.

Right-Versus-Right Dilemmas
• truth versus loyalty
• individual versus community
• justice versus mercy
• short-term versus long-term

Right-Versus-Wrong Dilemmas

These decisions are generally fairly clear-cut. The right answers for those with a conscience are not hard to find. Kidder suggests a three-part test for right-versus-wrong decisions:
1) Is it illegal?
2) Is it dishonest?
3) Is it immoral?

---

[2] Kidder's paradigm is a good pedagogical model for analyzing the decision-making process and reflecting on values and personal choices for self-understanding. However, there are some problems with the paradigm. For example, if any act that is dishonest is wrong, then any truth versus loyalty decision is a right-versus-wrong rather then a right-versus-right dilemma. According to the paradigm, opting for loyalty over honesty would result in a dishonest act and therefore a wrong choice.

If the answer to any of these questions is yes, the decision is a wrong one.

According to Kidder's paradigm, it is immoral to renege on a duty or fail to uphold an established moral value. When the desire to win is greater than the desire to do the right thing, there is a strong temptation to make immoral decisions. Winning is not a "four-letter word," and valuing winning does not mean you are an immoral person. But as the emphasis on winning becomes more important, the temptation to act inconsistently with your moral values becomes stronger. When behaving in accordance with your moral values is given second priority to winning, the lessons players learn change dramatically.

Right-Versus-Right Dilemmas

Kidder subdivides right-versus-right dilemmas into four types of decisions. They are considered moral dilemmas if the decision involves moral values. "Right versus right" means that there is no wrong answer, regardless of how the dilemma is resolved. In other words, there would be no illegal, dishonest, or immoral action. How the dilemma is resolved depends on how the values are prioritized and the reasoning process that is used. Working through right-versus-right decisions is a great way to learn more about what is important to us. These four dilemmas will be used to work through some decision-making examples in a sport context.

Truth Versus Loyalty

Juan, the captain of the baseball team, returned late Friday night to check the field for the game on Saturday morning. While he was walking to his car, he noticed lights on in the computer laboratory. Although he wasn't sure, it looked like Jim, the starting pitcher, along with someone else who didn't look familiar. In a hurry to get home, Juan jumped into his car. As he pulled out, he noticed that Jim's car was in the parking lot.

The next day, Juan learned that several computers had been stolen from the lab. Not sure what to do, Juan went to Coach Johnson and told him what he had seen. He asked the coach not to divulge where he got the information.

There are many difficult questions here. Should Coach Johnson divulge the information (or encourage Juan to go to the school principal) or keep it to himself? This dilemma pits the coach's loyalty to his player against being honest about what happened Friday night. To whom does the coach owe allegiance? Is it the school, the team, or his players? Is loyalty to his player more important than being honest?

The answers to right-versus-right dilemmas such as this one are rarely easy to sort out. There always seem to be gray areas, depending on what values are more important. To confound the issue, there are often other values involved that affect how the central issue is viewed. In this scenario, the loyalty-and-honesty issue between coach and player is complicated by the question of the coach's primary responsibility, and what obligations, if any, he has for the confidentiality of the player who came to him.

Individual Versus Community

Mary, the second-string point guard on the basketball team, has a scholarship opportunity. A scout from the college calls the coach to say that Mary is one of two finalists for a scholarship and that they are sending a scout to watch Mary play that afternoon. Obviously, this will help the school make their final decision. However, Coach Evans had not planned on playing Mary in this important play-off game. The team's best chance at making the state finals is with the starting point guard. Coach Evans does not know what she should tell the scout about coming to watch Mary play.

Although this dilemma does not directly involve two different moral values, it requires the coach to prioritize the needs of the individual against the good of the team. Kidder terms this type of dilemma individual versus community. What is in the best interest of the team? Is going to the championship most important? Would this goal be compromised if the coach were to play the second-string guard? Had the coach not kept her priorities clear in the past and had winning seasons, would there even be a scholarship opportunity for Mary? What about the coach's loyalty to Mary?

Justice Versus Mercy

Chris has been a starting center for four years. The team's offense is run around him. He has been a team leader and he has followed the team rules. The night before the game with the arch rival school from across town, Chris gets in a fight with a player from the rival school and sends him to the hospital. Chris has been arrested on an assault charge. He is released from custody under his parents' recognizance and is in school. His court date is weeks away.

Team rules require that players remain in good standing in the school and community in order to stay on the team. According to the rule, anyone who is not in good standing will be let go from the team. Should Chris be kept on the team?

Playing on a team is a privilege. In order to have that privilege, players must follow the rules. If the rules are violated, there are consequences that apply to all. Consistency of rule application is a fundamental principle of child rearing, teaching, coaching, and law enforcement. But the only real rule about rules is that there are exceptions. Everyone makes mistakes, and the consequences should fit the crime. Chris has had an exemplary record with the team. He has never exhibited a quick temper, been thrown out of a game for excessive fouls, or received a technical foul. His self-control has been more than commendable. The coach has considered him a role model for the younger players.

Clearly Chris is not in good standing in the community. Based on a literal interpretation of the team rule, he is in violation. The purpose of the rule was to motivate players to walk away from trouble. Chris did not do that. Should the coach throw Chris off the team, suspend him pending the outcome of the court date, or allow him to play until the court date? Are Chris's past behavior and positive contributions to the team factors to be weighed in making the decision? Should the coach make an exception and show mercy or does justice dictate consistent application of consequences?

Short-Term Issues Versus Long-Term Issues

Anna was on the vaulting runway. She had two vaults. With a 6.5 the team would take first place. She was the last competitor for the team and all eyes were on her. As she landed the first vault she knew she was in trouble. She immediately fell to the mat, holding her knee. As she stood up to leave the mat, she realized that she could not completely straighten out her knee. Coach Wu rushed over to check on her athlete. The score flashed up. Anna had received a 6.2, which would drop the team down in the final standings. Anna was clearly in pain and could not walk without a limp. She looked at the coach. What should the coach do?

If Anna's injury is only minor, taking her second vault may delay her recovery time but will not cause any permanent problems. On the other hand, if the injury is more serious, running down the runway and landing a second vault could cause permanent long-term damage to her knee. Is 17-year-old Anna capable of making the decision to vault again at that moment? Should the coach make the decision for Anna, knowing both the long-term and short-term potential repercussions for Anna and the team?

Three Types of Reasoning: Which Works for You?

Most people have a decision-making method. Not everyone has specifically analyzed the method he or she uses, but it has evolved and been honed subconsciously over time. For some people, the way they reason may change depending on the type of decision involved or the particular facts and circumstances. Kidder (1995) has taken three traditional approaches to moral reasoning and described them in a very practical and understandable way.

Ends-Based Reasoning

This type of reasoning evaluates the outcomes of decisions. It examines how a decision and its resulting course of action will affect others. The "right" answer is the one that does the greatest good for the greatest number of people. Thus, there are two factors weighed in this type of decision-making: the greatest good today and in the future, and the greatest number of people positively affected. The values are not as important as the consequences of the decision. If the dilemma occurred at a different time and the consequences were different, the decision might be different.

People who engage in ends-based reasoning tend to see issues as gray rather than black or white. Particular facts, circumstances, emotions, and gut feelings are viewed as legitimate factors that may influence the decision-making process. This type of decision-maker would not make a good referee. Referees make instantaneous decisions based on the literal interpretation of the rules, regardless of how it will affect the outcome of the game. On the other hand, medical doctors generally assess the pros and cons of treatments for a patient, taking into consideration the outcome of each of the options. The correct decision for one patient might be a less-desirable option for another with the same disease.

Rule-Based Reasoning

On the opposite end of the spectrum is rule-based reasoning. According to rule-based reasoning, the fundamental principle upon which moral decisions are based is nonnegotiable and inflexible. No consequence can justify a violation of the fundamental value or rule, which is that all people must be treated the same way. The term for this concept is *universality.* The core principle is that all persons should be treated with respect for their dignity and self-worth.

In addition to universality, rule-based decision-making must be *impartial* and *consistent* across dilemmas and situations. Correct decision-making must result in actions that treat everyone the same way, regardless of the outcome or consequences. Referees apply the game rules equitably and strive to treat all players the same.

Care-Based Reasoning

Care-based reasoning is based on the golden rule "do unto others as you would have them do unto you." It is rooted in empathy for someone else. It requires that decision-makers put themselves in the place of the object of the decision. Asking "How would I feel if this were done to me?" makes for a care-based test of reciprocity. In some dilemmas there may be more than one object, which can make the decision more complex. In these cases, the decision-maker has to determine which person(s) should receive the projected feelings of empathy.

Many religious codes of behavior rely on this fundamental principle. Although some philosophers do not consider care-based reasoning a philosophical approach to decision-making, for some people this can be the fundamental principle that guides their decision-making.

Which Reasoning Process Is Right for Coaches?

Is there a correct way for coaches to reason? The answer is no. Although officials are hired to use rule-based reasoning, the job description of a coach offers no such easy answer. You will probably identify with one reasoning process over others, but most people use different processes in different situations. The only criteria for a good coach is to reflect on the decision-making process and care about maintaining a positive learning environment for the players. Any of the reasoning processes can result in sound leadership decisions and actions, as long as the coach has communicated the expectations, rules, and basic priorities for decision-making to the players.

Perhaps looking at one of the examples through the different types of reasoning will help you identify your preference. Actually, you do not need a preference, as it is often helpful to think through difficult decisions using all three types of reasoning before making a final decision and taking action. Take the example of Chris, the player arrested for assault the night before the big game.

First, it must be pointed out that if the coach decides to play Chris just because the chances of winning are better, this takes the decision out of the right-versus-right paradigm. Winning is not a moral value. The values being weighed would be winning versus justice. While there is no sure way to know the coach's motivations, the action will be clear to all and inferences will be made. Thus, if the coach keeps Chris on the team and allows him to play, the reasons need to be made clear to the team.

The coach may also want to revisit the "no fighting" rule, since both aggressor and recipient are subjected to the same disciplinary action. Sometimes the appropriateness of a rule is only examined after a situation develops that raises the question. Changing the rule might be in the best interest of justice.

Ends-Based Reasoning

Using ends-based reasoning, the consequences of each decision are weighed to determine which produces the greatest good for the most people. If Chris plays, the team and the school benefit from the playing strength he brings to the court. If Chris does not play, the team suffers the consequences. If Chris is subsequently found guilty, the season is over, and removal would have no practical consequence. If Chris is found innocent of the assault charge, justice prevails, at least on the issue of his standing in the community and school.

Chris's involvement in a physical altercation is also against the team rules. He will be guilty of this regardless of the outcome in court. However, given his history of exemplary behavior, it is likely that he did not provoke the fight and acted in self-defense. Given these facts and circumstances, an ends-based thinker might conclude that the greatest good is served by allowing Chris to play.

Rule-Based Reasoning

The notions of fairness and justice are central criteria for decision-making using rule-based reasoning. According to the community, school, and team rules, Chris's involvement in a fight is grounds for removal from the team. In the interest of fairness and justice to all team members who break rules, Chris should not be allowed to play. The principles of impartiality and consistency require that the rules be applied to Chris regardless of the consequences. For a rule-based thinker, this decision is probably an easy one, and Chris is removed from the team roster immediately.

Care-Based Reasoning

Care-based thinkers are going to put themselves in Chris's shoes and ask, how would I feel if this were me? Anyone who is physically attacked has the right to defend himself. Someone using care-based reasoning would probably feel compassion for Chris and believe that mercy was the right decision. However, once the exception has been made, the intent behind the action is subject to opinion. For example, some may feel that the coach didn't make the decision out of compassion for the player, but because of the desire to win.

Conclusion

The decision-making paradigm, the types of reasoning processes, and the scenarios presented in this chapter were introduced as ways to analyze the decision-making process. More important than any definitive answers or solutions to the dilemmas are the reasoning processes used to arrive at those decisions. When difficult decisions are analyzed, the reasons for them become more clear. It is often the motivation for decisions and the intent behind actions that reveal our values most clearly.

PART II

Scenarios Involving Individual Players
Coaching Decisions, Actions, and the Messages They Send

INTRODUCTION

In Part II, some hypothetical case scenarios of common coaching problems are presented. The scenarios focus on issues that involve individual players. The purpose of the scenarios is three-fold. First, a template is presented that can be used as a guide for analyzing problems and developing options to handle situations. It is analogous to a lesson plan template for planning a team practice, except that it is designed for planning a meeting with an individual player. Second, the scenarios and template provide an opportunity to examine the communication process with the athlete during the meeting. Third, the scenarios provide an opportunity for discussion of the values that undergird coaches' decisions, actions, and the messages they send to athletes.

In order to provide realistic contexts for the scenarios, names and sexes were assigned to the players and coaches. In some of the cases, the assignment was arbitrary and in others it was assigned to prompt discussion of gender-specific issues. For example, in the scenarios dealing with applying team rules consistently, criteria for the starting lineup, undermining behavior, and academic honesty, the sex of the player and coach were chosen arbitrarily. In the author's experience as a coach educator, these problems seem to occur with equal frequency on male and female teams and are problems for both male and female coaches. Although the author assigned genders in the scenarios, the author did not intend to suggest that the problems—with the exception of the pregnant athlete—are indigenous to that sex. Rather, gender assignments were made to provide a specific and realistic context for discussion.

During a season, coaches spend many hours with their athletes in an environment that can be intensely focused and highly competitive. Typically, school teams practice five days a week for two hours a day. Coaches often work with the same team for several years. Given the amount of time they spend with their athletes, it isn't surprising that coaches get to know their players more personally than many other adults. When players are treated fairly and consistently, over time they develop a rapport with their coach that develops into a trusting relationship. It isn't surprising that players often feel comfortable going to the coach with problems that they may not be comfortable discussing with parents, teachers, or other adults in their lives.

Coaches, not Counselors

Although most coaches do not have training in counseling, they often find themselves working with athletes in one-on-one situations. Sometimes the issues involved are directly related to the team, but at other times the problems are personal in nature. In either case, coaches need to handle situations as they arise. The template and scenarios presented in Part II provide coaches with a guide for dealing with some of the more challenging problems that coaches can encounter. However, coaches need to know their limitations. The most appropriate thing to do in many cases is to seek advice from someone with the training and background to handle the problem or directly refer the player to a trained professional. Particularly because coaches often have a very strong influence on their players, it is most important that they influence or counsel students only in areas that are appropriate. The NASPE National Standards for Athletic Coaches (1995) are a helpful guideline for delimiting the coach's role in the social/psychological area.

According to the standards, coaches need to recognize the unique needs of athletes, and support their growth as athletes as well as individuals, and provide support for the development of a balanced lifestyle outside the realm of sport. The standards in the social/psychological domain also advocate enhancing players' self-esteem through encouragement and positive interactions. As a coach, it is often difficult to draw the line between taking an interest in athletes, supporting their unique needs, and helping them over hurdles that may affect their short- and long-term goals on and off the field. This is an area that requires careful consideration and mature judgment.

Making decisions and establishing boundaries for coach-player relationships are not always easy because circumstances are often not clear-cut. Coaches who use the NASPE coaching standards as a guideline for appropriate areas of influence in athletes' lives and keep the shared values of the team as a community in the forefront will have an easier time appropriately dealing with difficult situations that arise.

Assumptions and Context for the Scenarios

The scenarios presented in Part II are based on the following assumptions:

- The players are at the high school varsity level.
- The school is in a competitive league and the athletic program reflects the school's educational mission.
- The coach would only dismiss a player from the team as a last resort.

Although the scenarios presented are for a competitive, high school varsity level, the issues are also common to junior high school and youth sport as well as some collegiate-level sport teams. Much as parents make decisions based on the developmental level of their children, so coaches' decisions need to be based on the appropriate developmental level and needs of the players they are working with.

As an intentional community, sport team involvement provides unique opportunities for coaches to positively influence players' character development. It also provides opportunities for the development of qualities that will help players become successful and productive members of their communities and prepare them for adult life in a competitive society. These outcomes, however, are not automatic by-products of sport experiences. They are products of the learning experiences designed and implemented by coaches and their vision of what the values of the next generation should be.

CHAPTER 5

The Template:
Your Guide to Problem Resolution

Do not say things. What you are stands over you the while, and thunders so that I cannot hear what you say to the contrary.

—Ralph Waldo Emerson

Table 5
Template for Planning

Analyzing the Issue
- Identifying the Problem
- Listing Inappropriate Behavior
- Determining What Action to Take
- Considering Possible Reactions by the Athlete

Setting up a Meeting with the Athlete
- Location and Physical Set-Up
- Arranging the Meeting
- Meeting Time
- Meeting Length

Outlining the Meeting
- Opening the Meeting and Presenting the Problem
- Taking Action
- Closing the Meeting

Considering Important Points

Scenario

A situation is presented that the coach must handle.

Analyzing the Issue

Identifying the Problem
The first step in resolving a situation is to define it clearly. State the behavior or issue that is problematic. Categorize the nature of the problem. For example:
- violation of a team rule
- moral/ethical behavior issue
- lack of motivation to work toward the team goals
- behavior affecting team unity
- criminal act

Listing Inappropriate Behavior
Describe the behavior that is problematic. Detail the effects the problem is having on the coach and/or team members. List the behaviors and incidents that have occurred in observable terms. It is very important to be as specific as possible. A general statement such as "You're not trying hard enough," doesn't convey a specific message and can be answered with a general "I'll try harder."

Determining What Action To Take
Your consequences or action is your bottom line. In thinking through what your action, if any, will be ask yourself the following questions:
- What is the purpose of meeting with the athlete?
- What consequences, if any, will there be if the problem persists?
- Is there an immediate consequential action you plan to implement?
- Is your bottom line dependent upon what the athlete says or how he or she reacts?

Depending on the nature of the problem and your purpose for the meeting, a plan of action may fall into one of the following categories:

- open communication lines to discuss a possible personal issue
- warning
- verbal reprimand
- specific consequence, i.e., not starting, less game time, benching
- suspension
- removal from the team

Considering Possible Reactions by the Athlete

Brainstorm every conceivable reason the athlete could have for his or her behavior. Anticipate the possible reactions he or she may have at the meeting. Will any reasons or reactions affect how you handle the problem? Think through what might change any repercussions you are thinking of using to handle the problem.

Setting Up a Meeting With the Athlete

Location and Physical Set-Up

The location sets the tone for the meeting. Determine whether it will be held in the office, the gym, a hallway, or outdoors on the playing field.

The physical set-up of the meeting space is also an important consideration. How do you physically set up the meeting area? Depending on the tone you want to set, there are several options.

Formal: Barrier (desk) between coach and player. Maximum authoritative position is with the coach standing and the player sitting.

Semi-formal: Coach and player at right angles. A chair next to desk for the athlete and coach at desk is an example of this set-up. Usually in this set-up the coach is sitting.

Informal: No barrier, sitting or standing face-to-face with athlete.

There are other considerations. Is the meeting private, behind a closed door, or is the door open with another coach/teacher present or in the vicinity? Is the meeting in the open but away from others so that you are in public view? Meetings with an athlete of the opposite sex should be carefully planned in regard to public view considerations.

Arranging the Meeting

How you arrange the meeting should be consistent with your plans and intentions. It is part of setting up the conditions. Do you ask the athlete to stop by after practice in a concerned way? Or do you say, "I'll see you in my office," in a stern voice?

Meeting Time

Consider when the meeting will take place. Should it be before, during, or after practice? Would it be more effective the next day? Do you want to deal with the problem immediately or do you want the athlete to have time to think about the meeting?

Meeting Length

There are no hard and fast rules for meeting length. Some problems require more time than others. In general, problems that deal with breaking rules or undermining authority take less time than personal problems or issues that are not as clear-cut and require discussion or explanation. Your basic personality and coaching style will also affect how long a meeting will take. A democratic coach might feel more discussion is important, while a more autocratic coach might want little or no discussion. The following time guidelines are suggested to help plan the meeting:

Short: One-way communication with limited discussion—about five to seven minutes.

Medium: Some two-way discussion, but focused on transmission of coach's decision for action–generally about 10 minutes.

Long: Extended discussion of a complex issue—time varies—12-20 minutes. May need follow-up or multiple meetings.

Outlining the Meeting

Opening the Meeting and Presenting the Problem

Consider what tone and body language you will use to start the meeting. Will you be authoritative, compassionate, business-like, or easy going? How will you approach the issue? What will you do (physically and verbally) to create the perception you want the athlete to have during the meeting?

Specifically identify the behavior or problem that needs to change. Define inappropriate behavior and provide examples. If an inappropriate behavior occurs in the meeting, point it out immediately. Refer to behavior, rather than using nonspecific and subjective terms like "attitude." For example, "You have a poor attitude" means to many athletes, "The coach doesn't like me." On the other hand, saying "You have been late twice and have criticized other players' stick work during practice" is more objective and is interpreted by more athletes to mean "I have some behaviors that the coach does not like that I need to change."

Focus on the behavior, not the person. Particularly when discussing skill or playing ability, whenever possible, focus on what the athlete needs to do, rather than criticize what he or she is not doing.

If the nature of the problem warrants it, allow the athlete time to discuss his perceptions regarding the issue and/or problem. This gives you a chance to understand and evaluate the athlete's reaction. If you have several options for the bottom line, the athlete's reaction may be necessary to determine what action the coach will take.

Taking Action

The action you will take to deal with the issue can range from a discussion with the athlete to a warning or consequences. The action a coach takes is often referred to as the "bottom line." It is helpful to anticipate as many circumstances as possible that may affect the action you will take. In some situations, it may be helpful to plan several options and make the final decision on your action during the discussion with the athlete. In some situations, nothing the athlete might say will alter the action you planned to take prior to the meeting. It is possible that the consequences may not be affected by the athlete's dialogue with you, but your demeanor or phrasing may be changed depending upon issues that emerge during the meeting.

However, if something comes up in the meeting that makes you question your anticipated action, take a "time-out." You may need time to determine facts, motive, evidence of remorse (or lack of it), etc., in order to make a final decision. Close the meeting, give yourself time to think through the new factors presented, and schedule another meeting.

Closing the Meeting

Take the lead in terminating the meeting. There are a number of ways to do this. General statements such as "I hope we can move forward positively from here. I'll see you at practice." are good closing statements but do not summarize the meeting. Particularly when the coach has given consequences for another incident, it is a good idea to restate what the consequences will be if there should be a reoccurrence. This statement needs to be a specific summary of the understanding reached. An example of this type of statement might be, "I know you can get to practice on time if playing is really important to you. I don't want to have to bench you, but if you are late again that is what I will have to do. It is up to you. Any questions?"

To close the meeting, the coach can stand up, gesture, or look at the door and move in that direction. The tone and type of closure will often depend on the nature of the issue and what the general outcome of the meeting was. If the player really did not seem to get the message and was resistant, the closure should reiterate the repercussions of noncompliance. Whenever possible, end the meeting leaving the athlete feeling positive and motivated.

Considering Important Points

This section in each scenario will discuss the impact of some of the decision-making alternatives, how the decision reflects the coach's values, the message the coach's action sends to the players, and in some cases, the current research findings pertinent to the issue.

Fairness:
Applying Team Rules Consistently

Jamal, a runner on the cross-country team, wants to do his conditioning on his own time several days a week. He has been running with a private track club year-round, and the school practices are conflicting with the private team workouts and practice schedule. He would like to compete in the school meets and attend practices when it does not conflict with the private club schedule. He has requested a meeting to discuss this with the coach.

Analyzing the Issue

Identifying the Problem

Assuming the coach has a team rule regarding attendance at practices, this athlete is asking for an exception to the rule. Without everyone at practice regularly, the sense of team unity, belonging, and interaction is affected. Jamal's request also forces the coach to set a precedent that requires

some justification or rationale to other players who may from time to time need exceptions.

Listing Inappropriate Behavior

Jamal has not missed practice, but he is asking the coach to allow him to practice several days a week with his private club team instead of with the school team.

Determining What Action To Take

The decision the coach makes on this one will depend on his values. If Jamal is a talented runner, the team could benefit from his participation in the win-loss column. If winning is what is most important, then a talented runner would be allowed on the team with such part-time participation.

However, if the coach views the team as a community, and if there are specific rules about attending practices to remain in good standing, then the coach needs to apply rules consistently in order to be fair and to maintain a healthy community. Is there room for compromise? It might be possible for the coach of the school team to incorporate some of the private club workouts into the school practices for Jamal. Individual sports do allow for some flexibility in practice workout schedules.

The way the coach handles this situation will reflect how his values have been stacked in importance. Even if everyone on the team agrees that Jamal should be allowed to compete, what is the message the team gets from the coach's actions? One message would be that exceptions to team rules will be made when winning is at stake. On the other hand, a coach who views the process as most important will have difficulty justifying exceptions to regular team participation.

Considering Possible Reactions by the Athlete

- Jamal decides not to run for the school team.
- Jamal agrees to talk to his private club coach, to discuss allowing him to practice with the school team for the entire season.
- Jamal decides to give up running for the private club. He runs for the school team.
- Jamal asks his two coaches to talk to each other and agree to a compromise that will allow him to be on both teams.

Setting Up a Meeting With the Athlete

When the athlete asks for a meeting, the coach should ask what the request concerns, in order to be able to think about it ahead of time. The setup can be semi-formal or formal, in the coach's office. The meeting will most likely be a short one, with the possibility of a follow-up meeting if the coach wants some time to consider the request or a compromise is to be considered.

Outlining the Meeting

Opening the Meeting and Presenting the Problem

In this situation the athlete is bringing the issue to the coach. The coach should listen respectfully to the athlete's entire request. Any questions or clarifications should be made prior to discussion. Depending on the coach's decision, he can either give an immediate answer or choose to think about it and give an answer at a later specified time.

Regardless of how outrageous the coach feels the request is, the tone during the meeting should be respectful of the athlete. In this initial meeting, the coach may ask what other activities and commitments Jamal has in his life. Sometimes athletes need help establishing realistic goals and prioritizing what is really important to them. Is Jamal committed to a long-term goal? How do his parents feel about his goals? It may be that Jamal really does not want to be on both teams, but his parents are pressuring him. He might actually be relieved with a "no" answer from the coach.

In any case, the coach can get some answers to these questions in the initial meeting. They may or may not influence the action taken, but asking questions and discussing these issues will indicate that the request has been respectfully considered and that the coach cares about Jamal as a person as well as a runner.

Taking Action

The coach either gives an answer or gives Jamal a specific time when there will be an answer. If the coach chooses to meet with, or talk to, the other team's coach, a time frame should given to the athlete.

Closing the Meeting

Both coach and athlete need to understand the process that will be worked out to resolve the issue. Unless Jamal has clearly decided to quit the school team, the concluding remarks should stress a positive attitude toward the resolution.

Considering Important Points

Fairness. Although a cross-country team often focuses on individual rather than team performance, if there is a team score, then it is a team sport. Assuming that there are limited entries for each team, if Jamal is allowed to run in the meets, it could mean someone else on the team is not running. Therefore, fairness could be an issue. If an exception is made for this student, why not make an exception for another student with a special academic program or family conflict?

Benefits. But what about the win-loss record of the community? Doesn't everyone benefit from being on a winning team? Couldn't the team's best interest be served by allowing this dedicated and talented athlete to run? If everyone on the team agrees to make him an exception, isn't that fair? This could be viewed as a right-versus-right dilemma—individual-versus-community. If everyone on the team agrees to allow him to run, even though he cannot practice with them regularly, then what is the conflict? It could be viewed as a win-win situation—the community benefits and so does the individual athlete.

Message. However, particularly when the player is talented, it is important to examine the message athletes receive when a coach asks the team to endorse an exception to an established rule. The coach is asking the players to prioritize the needs of the team above established rules for participation. Coaches may relieve their own guilt by putting the question to a team vote, but it does not change the message the players receive. Particularly when the player is a talented athlete, it is logical for others to assume that the motive for the exception is improving the team's win-loss record.

Responsibility. There are many potential positive outcomes of sport. They include respect for team rules, respect for other team members, contributing to a team effort, and being part of a cohesive unit. But they are not automatic by-products. The coach who wants to achieve these outcomes needs to structure the environment to promote them. Particularly in individual sports such as cross country, where the natural tendency is to treat the athletes individually, the coach who wants athletes to learn about being part of a team—both its responsibilities and its benefits—needs to emphasize the team aspects of the sport.

Involvement. Belonging and dedication to a community require involvement. Without involvement and commitment to shared values, there is no community. Rules and expectations are created to foster group goals and also to maintain the quality of life within the community. As a leader, the coach has to weigh the importance of the values underlying the action to be taken.

Individual Needs. The school coach could individualize Jamal's practice schedule enough to allow him to meet his private club team goals as well as the school team's criteria for participation. This would mean working with the private club coach to see if it is possible for Jamal to work out with the school team regularly and also fulfill his long-term physical training needs for his private club training.

Safety. Because of the need to peak and taper training schedules around competitive events, it may not be safe for an athlete to train for two different competitive schedules in the same season. Even if there was a way for Jamal to fit both the private club and school team practices in his schedule, the physical demands of double practices must be considered. Because of the dangers of overtraining, many athletic leagues and school districts have policies that prevent athletes from participating on more than one team during a season. Ultimately the well-being of the athlete should be the first consideration.

Approach. Another factor involved in the coach's decision is the approach that the athlete has taken in order to deal with the situation. Did he approach the coach prior to the season to discuss the conflict, or has this come up after several missed practices? Does the player show respect for the school team and its participants, as well as for the established rules and expectations? An athlete who feels automatically entitled to an exception because of his superior ability will probably not make a positive contribution to the team—except maybe in the win-loss column.

Commitment. One of the things we learn through life experience is to prioritize and juggle commitments. A key part of this process is choosing what and how many commitments to make. Is it better to have a broad base of experience or to focus on a particular activity in which to excel? Coaches who demand too much from athletes under the guise of "teaching them dedication" can prevent young people from experiencing a variety of activities during their developmental years. Often more important than the decision the coach makes is the motive behind it. A coach who demands excessive dedication may be motivated more by the need to win than the desire to teach the athletes about dedication.

Ability and Playing Time:
Criteria for the Starting Line-up

Mary, a senior who was a starting forward on the basketball team for three seasons, loses her starting position to Casandra, a more skilled freshman. She is having trouble dealing with her status as a nonstarting player and resents the fact that she lost her position. She seems to be turning others against Casandra. Her behavior is affecting team unity and morale. Mary makes an appointment to see the coach to discuss her nonstarting status.

Analyzing the Issue

Identifying the Problem

Mary displays a negative attitude during practice. She is good friends with the starting players and is doing whatever she can to keep them from accepting and working with Casandra. It appears as though Mary's friends are feeling pressured to sabotage Casandra's performance. Team morale and cohesiveness have decreased since the team's starting lineup was announced.

Listing Inappropriate Behavior
- Mary puts out less energy during drills than she did previously.
- Her body language while the coach is talking indicates resentment.
- She makes comments under her breath when the coach is talking.
- She often does not assist in putting away equipment.
- She appears to be bad-mouthing Casandra to the other starting players.

Determining What Action To Take

Taking Mary out of the starting lineup as a senior says a lot about the coach's values. A coach who values loyalty and commitment over skill would not start a freshman if skill levels were comparable. Since this coach started the more skilled player, her action indicates that skill is the primary criterion for starting. The coach needs to make a judgment about Mary's potential in order to determine the direction of the meeting.

Although it is not always easy to make these judgment calls, it is often necessary. It could be that Mary is just not working hard enough and that she could get her starting position back with more effort. In that case, identifying the areas that need work and encouraging Mary to work harder would be the focus of the meeting. On the other hand, if the difference in skill abilities is so great that the coach feels Mary cannot earn her spot back, she may want to handle the meeting differently.

If the coach believes that Casandra's skill is so far superior to Mary's that there is almost no chance for Mary to start, then it would be more compassionate to help Mary accept her new role. Encouraging her to work hard and building up her hopes of starting will only bring further disappointment, anger, and resentment. This would not be helpful to the team, to Mary, or to Casandra. Ultimately, Mary has to accept her new status on the team, whatever the coach indicates it will be. If the coach can give her an idea of the amount of playing time she will have, it may help her make the adjustment. It is understandable that she is upset and will need help dealing with her disappointment. However, she needs to deal with her anger, move past it, and make a positive contribution to the team. Mary needs to feel like she is still a valuable team member, even if that means as a substitute for a starting player.

Considering Possible Reactions by the Athlete

Mary comes to the meeting angry. Her body language and comments indicate that she believes she has been unfairly demoted to a nonstarting position.

- Mary denies that she is angry and hurt. She believes she is still giving 100 percent.
- Mary comes in very upset. She feels the coach owes her for her three years as a loyal team member. She is humiliated to be replaced by a freshman and is thinking of quitting the team if she is not going to start.
- Mary is angry and humiliated but wants to stay on the team. She is willing to try to accept her new role on the team and make a positive contribution to team unity.

Setting Up a Meeting With the Athlete

In this scenario, the player has made an appointment to see the coach. When a player asks for a meeting, it is often helpful to ask what it concerns. This gives the coach time to think about the issue before speaking with the player. In this situation, what Mary has on her mind is not difficult to project. The meeting can be semi-formal. Whether the meeting is held before or after practice will depend on how the coach anticipates Mary will respond to the coach's decision. If the coach feels the decision will be upsetting to Mary, it may be unrealistic to expect Mary to maintain a positive attitude throughout practice if the meeting is right before practice. Holding the meeting after practice would give Mary time to regain her composure.

Outlining the Meeting

Opening the Meeting and Presenting the Problem

Since Mary has asked for the meeting, she will probably confront the coach about her nonstarting status. In all probability, Mary's self-esteem has taken a blow. Since she was a starting player for three seasons, it is likely that the decision has humiliated and angered her. The meeting will probably be an emotional one. When a player is angry, it is easy for the coach to become defensive. The coach will be most effective if she lets Mary know that she is empathetic and understands how she feels.

Mary will want to know why she isn't starting. When outlining the reasons for the decision, the coach should try to preserve her dignity. Since Mary was a starter for three seasons, she also started as a freshman. It is possible that she took the place of a senior too. Pointing this out may make Mary feel less humiliated. In an attempt to justify the decision, if the coach becomes defensive, it is easy to overstate the reasons. Using game statistics and objective criteria is better than making subjective generalizations. Care should be taken not to compare Mary's strengths and limitations to Casandra's—or any other player.

Finally, the coach needs to open the discussion about Mary's behavior. Her lack of energy, negative comments under her breath, and talking about Casandra to the other players have to be addressed. Mary needs to understand the impact her behavior is having on the team unity and morale.

Taking Action

The more specific the coach can be about Mary's future role, the better for everyone—Mary, the coach, and the team. Mary needs to know if she will have playing time. No promises should be made if this is not a strong possibility. The coach needs to let Mary know that she can still make a strong contribution both on and off the court—that she is still an important part of the team.

Once the coach has given Mary the reasons for the decision, and her new role on the team has been discussed, Mary needs to decide whether she can handle it and continue to make a positive contribution to the team. She is a valuable team member, but she needs to be positive and supportive of everyone on the team—including Casandra.

The bottom line is, if Mary cannot change her attitude and accept her new role on the team, the coach may want to help her find something more positive to do with her time. Continuing with the team would not be a positive experience. Helping Mary make that decision and allowing her to leave the team with dignity might be best for everyone. This decision and discussion may be better in a follow-up meeting after Mary has had some time to adjust to her new status. This is a judgment call the coach can make as the meeting progresses.

Closing the Meeting

The coach needs to let Mary know how valuable she has been to the team. Depending on how the athlete responds during the meeting, the coach should either be optimistic about her adjustment and future role, or let her know that she will respect whatever decision she makes. If Mary chooses to stay on the team, she needs to put the past behind her and act positively toward the team, her teammates, and her new role. It isn't necessary to threaten Mary with repercussions if she continues her negative attitude. If she continues to undermine team unity and Casandra's relationship with her teammates, the coach can meet with her again.

Considering Important Points

Starting. The coach may not view starting as a status symbol. However, most players perceive starting as a benchmark of their ability and value to the team. If the coach does not see the starting lineup as a status symbol and the players do, there may be a mismatch between values that can lead to problems. Players expect to be treated fairly. Even when they know the criteria for starting, they can be intensely disappointed when they are not selected. The disappointment is compounded, and the coach may be perceived as unfair, if they do not understand the reasons for the coach's actions.

Criteria. Thus, the criteria for playing time should be clearly communicated to the team at the beginning of the season. Depending on the level of competition, the options can range from equal playing time for everyone on the team to playing the most-skilled players at all times. Basing decisions on pre-established criteria provides consistency and is important for developing a sense of trust between the players and coach. The parents need to be made aware of these criteria as well. It is a good idea to include this information in a letter or meeting with the parents, which can be done in conjunction with the team rules and expectations.

Loyalty. When players join a team, they are expected to be loyal, dedicated, and to give 100 percent. Given these expectations, it isn't surprising that players who spend three years on a team, particularly with the same coach, expect their loyalty and dedication to be reciprocated. Loyalty often has an expensive, but unwritten, price tag, and it is often given priority over many other core values. Some coaches would never start a freshman over a senior regardless of ability or personal attributes.

Judgment. When coaches hold tryouts or choose their starting lineup, they must make judgment calls about players' ability and potential. Even with objective selection criteria, a player's potential is a subjective judgment. In this scenario, the coach had to make a judgment about Mary's potential. If, in the coach's mind, no amount of hard work could make Mary as good as Casandra, then meeting with Mary and encouraging her to work to get her starting spot back would be setting her up for failure. If the coach believed that Mary was not going to start or have much playing time, then meeting with her before the public humiliation of finding out when the starting lineup was announced would be more compassionate.

Options. What about the coach's decision not to start a senior? Mary's reaction to her demotion is predictable. Another option is to put her in the starting lineup and substitute Casandra. This allows Mary to keep the starting status, but the coach could give more playing time to the freshman. If Casandra understands that the starting spot has to be earned, this might be a feasible compromise.

Skill. Finally, what about starting a freshman player whose skill is unequivocally better than a senior's? Or what about a freshman whose personal attributes such as height, strength, or speed far surpass anyone's on the team? Is it fair to deny that player a starting position if skill has been the main criterion for starting?

Is there an unwritten rule that players must pay their dues before they earn a starting role on a team?

Coaches who clearly communicate the criteria for playing time at the beginning of the season will minimize the number of problems that occur. When playing time is based on ability, however, even when the criteria are clear, disappointments are inevitable. Although it is not a lesson anyone looks forward to, learning to deal effectively with disappointment is a life skill. Coaches who can empathize with players' feelings will be more likely to communicate with them in a sensitive way and help them learn to accept their limitations with dignity, adjust their goals, and continue moving forward.

SCENARIO 3

Respect for the Coach:
Undermining Behavior During Practice

Jack, the starting 3rd man on the lacrosse team, is very
critical of the coach. He has an opinion about most things,
particularly the organization and content of the practices.
During practices, his sarcastic and derogatory comments
are made so that the coach and the rest of the team can
hear them.

Analyzing the Issue

Identifying the Problem

Derogatory comments in public are disrespectful, demeaning, and hurtful. In this situation, Jack's comments will negatively affect the group and set the tone for a climate of disrespect during practice. The behavior undermines the coach's leadership, is distracting to everyone, and does not promote a fun or supportive atmosphere.

If it is allowed to continue, the coach could lose the players' respect and confidence; productivity during practice would be compromised as well. It could also lead to team members being disrespectful to each other.

Listing Inappropriate Behavior

Making judgmental comments:
- "This drill sucks!"
- "Do we really have to? What a waste of time!"
- "My grandmother knows more about the game than he does."

Using body language that indicates disrespect:
- Rolling his eyes during explanations.
- Talking while coach is speaking.
- Walking away when spoken to.
- Throwing up his hands at a call made by the coach.

Determining What Action To Take

Regardless of our intent, how what we say affects others is important. There are differences between being honest to keep communication lines open and being disrespectful, undermining, or hurtful. Basic respect for other people's feelings and respect for the coach as a person and an authority figure are essential for the health and productivity of the team as a community. Whether the goal is to improve, to play well, to win, or to have fun, behavior toward others needs to be respectful. The bottom line is that the undermining behavior must stop. But what is the best way to get the intended result?

The coach should talk to Jack about his behavior as soon as possible. However, care should be taken not to do what the player has done, which is to publicly humiliate someone. "Fighting fire with fire" is not a good solution. This is an opportunity for the coach to demonstrate how to treat someone else with respect and dignity.

At the time of the inappropriate comments, the coach may have to say or do something immediately to stop the behavior. The goal of this initial communication should only be to end the episode. This could mean giving the player an extended look, asking him to stop, or changing what the team is doing—perhaps sending the team for a quick sprint. If the initial effort is not successful, sending the team for a run and speaking directly with the player without the rest of the team present is a possible alternative. This should be done without embarrassing him or being disrespectful in response to his disrespect.

In order to create an atmosphere of trust and respect for others, the coach must demonstrate respect for the players. Immediately pulling the player off to the side and addressing the specific inappropriate behavior is a good first step. If the behavior continues, dismissing him from participation with a follow-up private meeting time is another possibility.

Considering Possible Reactions by the Athlete
- Jack continues the disrespectful behavior during the meeting.
- Jack comes to the meeting with a new and respectful attitude.
- Jack says he is quitting the team.
- Jack does not come to the scheduled meeting but is in school.

Setting Up a Meeting With the Athlete

If management techniques during the episode do not stop the behavior, the coach may want to ask the player to leave the court and schedule a private meeting after practice. If the behavior stops during practice, but the coach wants to discuss it with the player, a follow-up meeting can be scheduled. It can be held immediately, or it may be scheduled for the next day, giving the athlete time to think about his behavior. Using a formal set-up in the coach's office is generally effective with players who are undermining authority. Unless the player is not clear about what behaviors are appropriate and what are not, the meeting will probably be a short one.

A private meeting before or after practice gives the coach a chance to help Jack learn about respect. Since undermining behavior deals with power and control issues, how and when the athlete gets a chance to speak should be carefully considered. The coach needs to be sure that the player understands the structure of the meeting, the boundaries between coach and player, and the seriousness of the problem.

When the player is allowed to speak, he should do so with tone, body language, and a message that is respectful. The coach may have to provide feedback during that meeting that lets him see what message he is sending and what adjustments he needs to make. If this can be done firmly but in a supportive way, the long-term relationship between coach and player will probably be more positive.

Outlining the Meeting

Opening the Meeting and Presenting the Problem

The tone of the meeting should be firm but optimistic. It will set the stage for a respectful and positive coach-player relationship in the future. With a player who oversteps boundaries, it is important that the coach establish and maintain control of the meeting. The specific inappropriate behavior should be outlined to help the player understand what behavior is acceptable and what is not.

Taking Action

The severity of the consequences would be at the coach's discretion. It is important that the athlete leave the meeting understanding exactly what behaviors are inappropriate, and what the repercussions for future disrespectful behavior will be. Because this type of behavior deals with control and power issues, it is important that the coach be decisive and definitive about the consequences for reoccurrences.

Closing the Meeting

The player should know that if his behavior changes, his status on the team will not be jeopardized. If the athlete demonstrates respect during the meeting, the coach can give him a chance to speak and explain his feelings. Getting to this point in the meeting would be a good step, because the ultimate goal is for the coach and player to have a relationship based on mutual respect. It also would set the stage for the player to make a positive contribution to the team atmosphere in the future. On the other hand, the player must know that the coach will not tolerate disrespectful behavior toward anyone. A summary statement such as "You are a valuable team member, and I know I can count on you to help keep the team practices positive and productive" sets the tone for a positive relationship in the future.

Considering Important Points

Behavior. It is important that the coach keep the focus on behavior that was inappropriate, not on Jack as "a bad person." If Jack perceives that his relationship with the coach is unsalvageable, then it will be hard for him to become a productive and positive team member. The coach should emphasize how Jack needs to behave in order to be a valuable and productive team member. Providing specific examples of the inappropriate behavior is essential. Before a player can change his behavior, he must know what was inappropriate.

Respect. On the other hand, Jack must also be told what the consequences will be if he cannot act respectfully. If the coach is perceived as weak or ineffectual, it would not be surprising if Jack continued to display the behavior that led to the meeting in the first place. It is helpful if the coach knows how he is perceived by the athletes. Coaches who are very laid back and easy-going may need to take a more firm position with a player displaying this type of behavior than they might otherwise.

Team Rules. Team rules are boundaries for behavior much like the sidelines are boundaries for game play. Creating an atmosphere of mutual respect, fairness, fun, and goodwill can prevent behavior problems that undermine the atmosphere. The ideal situation is to create an environment that motivates players to behave in ways that are consistent with the shared values of the team. If the coach has articulated such values as respect, fairness, hard work, commitment, and honesty, and has created an atmosphere that fosters these values, then the number of times that serious repercussions are needed can be minimized.

Player Input. Some coaches feel that players should have input into the organization and content of practices, while others feel this is exclusively the coach's domain. (Extremely authoritarian coaches who do not allow players to have any input may want to examine the educational experience they are providing for their players). Players need to know how the coach feels about player input. In general, a player who has been disrespectful should demonstrate respectful behavior before being allowed to have input. Thus, the coach may want to let Jack know that if he demonstrates that he can behave respectfully, the coach will be open to feedback and constructive suggestions. However, Jack's suggestions should occur at an appropriate time and place. The saying "It isn't what you say, but how you say it," may be applicable in this scenario. Helping Jack learn respectful behavior toward others may be a lesson that will help him in other situations as well.

Boundaries and Influence. Sport is a good place for teaching about being part of a team, because most athletes want to play. Some students have not had an opportunity to be in a structured community such as a team, and they may need guidance to learn how to behave toward others. Either they will test the boundaries for behavior, or the team values won't be apparent enough for them to pick up on without some individual guidance. For these players, a private meeting with the coach can help make the expectations clear. For others, athletics is what keeps them coming to school and maintaining a passing grade-point average. Coaches have influence because athletes want to play, and clearly defined boundaries and consequences for noncompliance are very effective motivators. However, the ability to influence these students is gone once they are dismissed from a team. If it is possible to resolve issues without resorting to this ultimate bottom line, it would be better and certainly more educational for the student.

In the most difficult situations, players come to the environment with such problems or character flaws that they cannot function in the group environment. In these circumstances, managing a player's behavior may require more than the coach can handle. The coach's goal is to help each player be a productive and successful team member. Deciding to dismiss a player from the team is a difficult decision. When a player's behavior is so problematic or disruptive that it compromises the team values, goals, or educational experience, then dismissal is a serious consideration. It is an individual-versus-community decision. Ultimately, the coach must weigh the needs of the individual against the impact that player's behavior will have on the team.

Honesty and Loyalty:
Academic Honesty and Athletic Eligibility

Angela, the highest scoring forward on the soccer team, was assigned a tutor when her math grades fell so low that her academic eligibility was threatened. Samantha, the team captain, comes to the coach and reports that Angela received the answers to a math test through an earphone during the exam. She asks the coach not to tell the team or the player who turned her in. The coach checks the test results, and Angela received the same score as her best friend and tutor, who took the exam at the same time. This corroborates Samantha's allegation.

Analyzing the Issue

Identifying the Problem

In this scenario, the coach and the team captain have allegiance to two overlapping communities—the team and the school. If the allegation is true, there are two problematic issues. First, Angela has been

dishonest; and second, she probably does not meet the academic eligibility standards to play.

This problem is compounded by the fact that the evidence is circumstantial. Although a student eyewitness to the earphone and the similar test results are strong evidence, they are only circumstantial. The earphone could have been an MP3 player or a hearing aid, and the similar answers could have been a result of studying together. A coach who wants to give a player the benefit of the doubt may hesitate to go to the teacher before checking the information and sources for dependability.

The immediate need of the team is to play its best athlete. Without Angela, the chances of a winning season are unlikely. There is also the issue of loyalty. For the coach, it is loyalty to the team members, the team goals, and the team rules. This allegiance conflicts with her loyalty to the teachers, who want to be fair to all students and prevent cheating on exams. For the captain, it is loyalty to a teammate and the needs of the team, weighed against honesty and upholding the academic eligibility standards.

Listing Inappropriate Behavior

The possibility of:
- Cheating
- Eligibility standards not being met

Determining What Action To Take

The coach could choose one of the following options:
- She can choose not to act on the information provided by the captain. Whether or not she believes the allegation, she can tell Samantha to keep the information to herself. This would mean no change in the Angela's status on the team.
- The coach can check with the math teacher to see whether Angela and her tutor had the same correct and incorrect answers. If the test papers are similar, the coach could decide to confront the player with her suspicions. Based on the outcome of this meeting, the student could be cleared of suspicion, asked to retake the exam in question, benched, suspended, or removed from the team.
- The coach can choose not to handle the problem di-

rectly, but to pass the information along to the athletic director or the next person in the chain of command. She also must decide whether to honor the captain's request for confidentiality, and determine the strength of the evidence with or without her information.

How the coach handles the captain's role in this situation also needs consideration. Formal due process (for serious sanctions) includes the right to face your accuser. If the eye-witness account of the earphone is necessary to find Angela guilty (resulting in removal from the team or suspension from school), then the coach has to decide whether or not to honor Samantha's request for confidentiality.

Considering Possible Reactions by the Athlete

- Angela is hostile and defensive and denies all allegations. She has reasons for the earphone (an MP3 player), and says that studying with the tutor explains the similar results.
- She denies all allegations of cheating and agrees to retake the test.
- She denies all allegations of cheating and refuses to retake the test.
- She admits that she cheated.

Setting Up a Meeting With the Athlete

The first decision the coach has to make is whether to act on the allegations. In the circumstances of this scenario, the math teacher has not challenged Angela's grade. Unless someone else comes forward with allegations of academic dishonesty, Angela is eligible to play. The coach first must decide whether Samantha's accusation is credible. Unless Samantha reports the incident to someone else in authority, the coach may choose not to act on the information. Another issue for the coach to resolve is Samantha's request for confidentiality. Confronting Angela will involve exposing Samantha as the source of the accusation. The coach will need to resolve this issue before taking action.

Some important factors for the coach to consider are: what is Samantha's motive for bringing the allegation to the coach? What, if anything, would Samantha personally gain if Angela was ineligible to play? How do Samantha and Angela get along as teammates? Is Samantha's decision to bring the allegation to the coach consistent with her past behavior as a team member and captain? If the answers to any of these questions lead the coach to question the veracity of Samantha's allegation, the coach may choose not to act on the information. Or, the coach may need to verify the information through independent sources.

If the coach chooses to confront Angela and wants her to retake the exam, this decision may be beyond her authority. The coach may need to discuss the situation with the math teacher, the athletic director, and/or a school administrator prior to meeting with Angela. If, for example, the coach decides to suspend the player until she has retaken the math test, but the administration wants her to play regardless of her academic standing, it would be counter-productive to choose this course of action. It is also possible that the math teacher would refuse to let Angela retake the test.

As soon as a course of action has been established that is agreeable to all involved personnel, the coach should contact the player and set up a meeting. She also needs to let Samantha know what the course of action will be if it involves her. Depending on what the coach decides to do, it may be that the meeting will include the math teacher or a school administrator. It is even possible that the coach may not participate in the meeting with the student.

Outlining the Meeting

Opening the Meeting and Presenting the Problem

If the coach holds a meeting with Angela, she should treat her respectfully regardless of her guilt or innocence. Short of a videotape of a crime in progress, the coach should keep in mind the possibility that Angela is innocent of the charge. Given the serious nature of the problem and the gravity of the possible consequences, the coach needs to keep her emotions in check. Although she may be upset and angry, it is important that she behave professionally, maintain control of her feelings, and deal with the athlete in a compassionate but firm manner.

Angela should be given the opportunity to tell her story and provide an explanation for the allegations against her. Particular care should be taken to allow her to maintain her dignity. When discussing the allegation, negative comments should be focused on the dishonest behavior, rather than on the player as a person. It is very likely that Angela will want to know who made the allegations. The coach needs to be prepared to handle this request.

Taking Action

Depending on the action decided upon by the coach and other school personnel, the player should have a clear understanding about the allegations against her, what her status as a player is, or when and how this determination will be made. If she is going to be asked to retake an exam, the date and information covered on the exam should be thoroughly explained. In the event that the player is being removed from the team, her right to appeal the decision to a higher authority should be explained.

Closing the Meeting

The player must leave with a clear understanding of the actions to be taken and her options regarding them. Regardless of the outcome of the meeting, she needs to be treated respectfully and her dignity preserved.

Considering Important Points

This scenario is multidimensional and deals with several core community values. How the coach stacks these values in importance will determine how she chooses to deal with the situation. Decisions concerning the importance of academic eligibility standards, honesty, and winning are compounded by the circumstantial nature of the evidence, the captain's request for confidentiality, and loyalties to overlapping communities.

Legality. There are also some important legal considerations. Denying a student the right to play an interscholastic sport based on inconclusive evidence may be grounds for a lawsuit predicated on denial of procedural due process and insufficiency of evidence. Thus, when dealing with more serious sanctions like removing a student from a team or declaring a student ineligible to play, coaches should check with the school administration for legal culpability before deciding on a course of action.

The legal doctrine of *in loco parentis* means "in place of the parent." This doctrine gives school personnel some latitude when dealing with student behavior and disciplinary sanctions. Particularly when disciplinary violations and their consequences are not serious, courts have allowed school personnel considerable discretion. When the allegations are more serious, the courts have generally used a sliding scale to determine the amount of procedural due process necessary for student disciplinary sanctions.[1] Sanctions such as school suspensions and expulsions have required maximum due-process procedures. More minor offenses have required as little as a statement of the charges and the sanction to be imposed. The courts have distinguished between the right to attend public school and the right to play interscholastic sports. Actions rendering students ineligible for sport participation generally have not required full due-process proceedings. However, particularly when a potential college scholarship may be at stake, greater due-process procedures may be needed.

Confidentiality. Due process is a factor for the coach to consider when deciding on the captain's request for confidentiality. If failing the math test would make Angela academically ineligible to play, due-process considerations may require disclosure of the person making the allegation and the specific evidence against Angela. Coaches should be careful not to promise confidentiality prematurely. Essential to the health of any team as a community is a sense of trust between the coach and players. This trust would be affected if the coach agreed to maintain confidentiality and subsequently had to renege on that promise.

For the coach who decides not to act on the captain's information because it would mean breaching confidentiality, there may be some proactive steps to prevent Angela from cheating on the next test. The coach could work with the math teacher, without divulging any specific information about the previous exam. This course

---

[1] In 1975, the U.S. Supreme Court ruled on the due process rights of public school students. It held that maximum due process for serious disciplinary violations calls for a written notice of the charges, the time and place of a hearing, a description of the procedures to be used at the hearing, names of the witnesses, the evidence that will be used against them, and the right to cross-examine witnesses. The accused also have the right to present their own witnesses and evidence. For further discussion of the legal parameters for students' due process rights see *Goss v. Lopez*, 419 U.S. 565 (1975).

allows the coach to maintain confidentiality and still take action to maintain academic and eligibility standards.

Academic Difficulty. Another possible alternative is to have Angela retake the test, either the same test or an alternate. If she is really having academic difficulty, another test covering the same material will probably demonstrate her overall achievement level. Choosing this course of action allows the coach to take action based on the new test results. This alternative does mean that the coach has to communicate her suspicions to the math teacher.

Eligibility. Academic eligibility standards are based on the premise that playing on an athletic team is a privilege that is earned by meeting the school's standards. One of the academic standards is a minimum grade point average that must be met in order to play. The team is really a community within a larger community, or a subset of the school community. Thus, the smaller community should reflect the values of the larger community. A coach who does not uphold the school's academic standards undermines the shared values of the school and team.

Loyalty. Decisions involving loyalty are almost always difficult. It is often easier to let loyalty to group goals become more important than loyalty and commitment to the group's shared values. This difficult choice can be a right-versus-right dilemma. However, when the decision involves protecting someone who has been dishonest, the decision is a right-versus-wrong decision.

Priorities. The way a coach chooses to handle the situation is indicative of her priorities. Coaches whose priority is to keep their players eligible will give their allegiance to the team's needs over honesty or the student's long-term academic interests. If the coach becomes a part of a cover-up, or does not take a proactive stand on maintaining the values of the group, the players will learn to give loyalty their highest priority, too. Without honesty as a fundamental value, the stability of the group and the educational foundation of the athletic team's experience are compromised. On the other hand, if the coach takes an action that upholds the academic eligibility standards and sends the message that all players, regardless of ability or importance to the team, will be subjected to the same standards, the players will have a clear understanding of what they have to do to play.

SCENARIO 5

Player Well-Being:
Pregnancy and Medical Eligibility

A sophomore and 16 years old, Marcia, the starting center on the basketball team, seems distracted and preoccupied. She has been in the locker room some mornings and the coach has heard her getting sick to her stomach. Her boyfriend has been hanging around and the coach has witnessed some intense conversations. The coach has also overheard some talk among the players that Marcia is pregnant. The team is undefeated and has its sights on the state championship, but it is still early in the season.

Analyzing the Problem

Identifying the Problem

Coaches are responsible for the physical and psychological well-being of their players when they are under their supervision. The problem in this scenario is, how much information does a coach need to take action and what action should be taken when the coach feels that a player's health may be at risk?

Listing Inappropriate Behavior

Marcia's lack of focus, morning sickness, and intense discussions with her boyfriend are not inappropriate behavior. However, these behaviors, coupled with the overheard conversation of her teammates, strongly suggest that Marcia's medical status may have changed since the season began and she was medically cleared for team participation.

Determining What Action To Take

If a coach feels that a player's medical status has changed since she was medically cleared for sport participation, and participation potentially puts her at risk, the coach has a duty to take appropriate measures to safeguard the athlete's health. A coach is not qualified to make medical eligibility decisions. Therefore, a coach who believes that an athlete's medical status has changed needs to be proactive and take action. The measures taken will depend on the legal mandates in the jurisdiction, the player's age, the specific circumstances of the situation, the league or school policies for athletic participation, and the coaches' professional judgment. For a player under the age of majority (which varies depending on jurisdiction), a coach's decision not to inform the parents of a suspected change in medical status could have legal ramifications. Compounding the problem in this scenario is the fact that the coach is making a judgment call on circumstantial facts. Ultimately, the coach must decide how much evidence is needed to take action and whether to notify the parents.

Taken together, morning sickness, preoccupation, lack of focus at practice, communicating intensely with a boyfriend, and overheard talk among teammates make a strong case for taking action. Even without all of this information, a coach may feel that action is warranted. The decision to inform the parents is a judgment call that the coach needs to think about very carefully. If the player is pregnant and is not allowed to play, the team loses its starting center. Because the repercussion affects the coach and team, it is not easy to make this decision objectively. One definition of a "professional" is an individual who puts the interest of the constituent above all other priorities—including self-interest. Although not all coaches are trained professionals, when dealing with children in an educational environment, coaches need to act professionally. However difficult, the best interests of the player should be the basis for coaching decisions.

Basketball is considered a contact sport and the season is a long one. Playing competitive basketball while pregnant involves potential physical risks to the mother and fetus. In any case, coaches are not medically qualified to determine the degree of risk involved. And, it would be inappropriate for the coach to decide for the player whether the risk is worth taking. So, regardless of the sport, once there is enough information to think a player's medical status has changed, the coach needs to take action.

Informing Parents

The decision to tell the parents is a difficult one for some coaches. Community values and standards vary from school district to school district. Some districts have policies and procedures in place for handling parental notification. It may be in the coach's best interest to talk to school or league administrators before taking any action. At the very least, coaches should apprise themselves of all applicable district policies, procedures, and state laws. Coaches' jobs have been jeopardized for far less-controversial decisions.

There are a number of ways the coach can handle notifying the parents. One is to let the school administrators handle the situation. This takes the problem out of the coach's hands completely. Although this option is politically the safest, some coaches would feel uncomfortable taking this action without communicating about it with the player first. Another option is to discuss the situation in a meeting with the player. In the meeting, the coach may suggest that they talk to the parents together, or perhaps have the player tell her parents before the coach talks to them. With this option, the discussion is not whether to inform the parents, but how.

If a meeting is held with the player, it is possible that the player will try to talk the coach out of notifying her parents, convince the coach that she isn't pregnant, volunteer to take a pregnancy test, or tell the coach that she will "take care of it." A coach who chooses not to inform the parents, or decides to allow the player to continue playing without medical clearance, is taking risks. These risks may jeopardize the player's or fetus' health as well as the coach's career. A coach may want to refer the player to a counselor who is qualified to help the athlete. It is inadvisable for the coach to be involved with any decision-making or solution regarding the pregnancy.

Considering Possible Reactions by the Athlete
Marcia:
- Denies she's pregnant.
- Quits the team.
- Admits she's pregnant and says she will "take care of it."
- Admits she's pregnant and has already told her parents.
- Begs you not to tell her parents and threatens to do something drastic if you do.
- Agrees to tell her parents with you.
- Agrees to tell her parents without you.

Setting Up a Meeting With the Athlete

Arrange the meeting as soon as possible after notifying the athlete. Under these circumstances, giving the athlete time to think about the meeting is not a good idea. The player is already under a great deal of stress, so the more quickly the meeting is held, the better. The coach should meet with the player in view of others but where they can talk privately.

Outlining the Meeting

Opening the Meeting and Presenting the Problem
It is appropriate to show compassion and concern for the player, however, the coach needs to maintain a professional demeanor. Opening the meeting by showing concern for the player's physical and emotional health is a good way to begin. The coach should present the reasons he believes the player's medical status has changed. The player should have the opportunity to provide explanations for, and discussion of, the reasons the coach has presented. If the player does not feel comfortable telling her parents, it is likely that the player will be emotional and angry with the coach's intrusion into her personal life. The coach needs to be prepared for this response.

Taking Action

Once the coach decides that there is enough evidence to believe that a player's medical status has changed, it would be hard for the player to totally change the coach's mind during the meeting. A coach is not qualified to make medical eligibility decisions. Unless the player has extraordinary explanations, the player will need to be medically recleared. For a player who is a minor, the parents should be informed. For players who are not minors, whether the parents are notified is a judgment call for the coach to make. This decision should be carefully considered before the meeting.

Closing the Meeting

Marcia needs to know that she can return to practices and full participation as soon as she has been recleared by a medical doctor.

Considering Important Points

Unique Relationship. Players typically develop a unique relationship with their coach. It is not unusual for players to spend several hours a day with their coach and teammates during the season. Some players spend more time with their coach than their parents. It isn't surprising that coaches are often privy to a lot more personal information about players than are other adults—even parents and relatives. Because the environment is less formal than the classroom, when coaches are perceived as approachable, players are often more comfortable discussing personal information with them than with other adults. Coaches who are perceived as caring and compassionate are often viewed as trustworthy too. Because of these qualities, players often feel safe talking about things happening in their lives around the coach or turning to the coach for advice about personal problems. If a coach has worked hard to develop a trusting and caring relationship with the players, then the decision to breach their confidence can be even more difficult.

Confidentiality. Although teachers and coaches are expected to keep grades, personal medical information, and performance-related evaluations about students confidential, they do not have the legally protected confidentiality status that attorneys have with clients or doctors with patients. The legal doctrine of *in loco parentis,* at least in theory, gives school personnel the latitude to work more informally with students and to act in their best interests without some of the legal "red tape." It does not give school personnel the right to work with the students independently of the parents. Hence, in the case of a suspected pregnancy, withholding this information from the parents, would not fall under the *in loco parentis* doctrine. Unless there was a very compelling reason, it would be hard to imagine circumstances that would allow a coach to suspend a player from team participation for medical eligibility reasons without informing the parents—particularly if the player was only 16 years old.

Legality. However, acting according to established legal parameters is not always consistent with what is perceived to be the most ethical or "right" thing to do. When coaches find themselves faced with a decision that involves acting outside established legal or school policy parameters, they need to weigh their decisions carefully. Sometimes a quick emotional response or acting on principle without careful thought does not produce the intended outcome. It can also end a coaching career. Under these circumstances, it can be helpful to discuss the situation with someone trustworthy before taking action.

Parental Notification. If the coach decides to inform the parents, how the coach chooses to work with the player to do this will depend on a variety of factors. Some considerations are: the maturity of the player, her relationship with her parents, the anticipated response of the parents, the community and school-district standards for personal behavior, the length of time the coach has known the player, the player's emotional stability, and the nature of the coach-player relationship in general.

The coach has to anticipate alienating the player by insisting that she be medically recleared to play and that the parents be told. Often, more approachable coaches tend to want to be liked by their players. For these coaches, forcing a player to tell her parents may be a very difficult thing to do. The option of waiting and allowing a player to talk to the parents without the coach's involvement is not without risk.

A player can be driven to desperate measures after meeting with the coach. It is foreseeable that the player could have an abortion or even attempt suicide. In serious personal situations such as this one, the recommended course of action is to refer the player to someone professionally trained to work with these types of situations, such as the school psychologist, guidance counselor, or nurse.

Planning. Once the coach decides that a player needs to be medically recleared, a plan needs to be made for communicating this decision to the player. If a coach has a meeting with the player and agrees to give her time to tell her parents, the coach needs to set a definitive timeline and feel sure that the player will not do something desperate. If the coach discusses the situation with the player and does not immediately contact a superior, the school psychologist, or the parents, the coach could face negligence charges if something were to happen to the player.

Since the tragedy at Columbine and other school violence occurrences, school districts may find themselves having to defend whether they are legally liable for school personnel not disclosing information that could have prevented injury. This decision can be a difficult one for the coach.

Follow Through. In the meeting with the coach, once Marcia realizes she cannot play without being recleared medically and her parents must be told, she may decide to quit the team. This may seem like the only way to avoid her parents finding out. It would not be wise for the coach not to follow through with telling Marcia's parents, even if she quits. Once the coach is sure enough to confront the player, it is necessary to act in the long-term best interests of the player.

Incorrect Assumption. Finally, there is the possibility that Marcia is not pregnant. The evidence on which the decision was made was circumstantial and required the coach to make a judgment call. In the long-term best interests of players, erring on the side of caution is prudent. However, once an allegation is made and the player had to tell her parents and have a bona fide pregnancy test for medical reclearance, the coach-player relationship will be strained at best. It is also possible that the parents will attempt to damage the coach's reputation or file legal charges for defamation of character.

Gender Issues. Male coaches of female teams need to be particularly careful when dealing with the personal problems of their athletes and meeting with them one-on-one. Particularly when problems have potentially life-altering consequences such as this one, even the most stable athlete can resort to desperate measures or behave unpredictably. Setting appropriate boundaries for discussions with players can prevent the coach from being drawn into personal conversations that are either inappropriate or could be misinterpreted if difficult situations were to develop later on.

Private conversations held with players can be held with an adult witness present (but out of earshot) or in a public place far enough away from others so as not to be overheard. With some players, coaches may want to have the conversation with a third party present (school personnel or teacher) or defer the conversation to the athletic director, school psychologist, or school nurse.

Respect for Others: Discrimination Based on Sexual Preference

The rumor is that Tom, the starting wide receiver on the football team, is gay. When confronted by his teammates, Tom has not denied the rumor, nor has he confirmed it. His answer is that what he does on his own time is his own business. Tom is a mature, quiet guy. Socially he has never been in the team's nucleus, but he was always accepted as one of the guys. Since the rumor started, Tom has not been playing well. His teammates do not want to be in the locker room with him, and he has been the subject of verbal abuse. The team's focus and unity has been adversely affected. They seem more focused on Tom's sexual preference than on the team goals.

Analyzing the Issue

Identifying the Problem

Sport teams are open to any member of the community who meets the eligibility and selection criteria. They provide a unique opportunity for young people to work toward a com-

mon goal with people who are different from themselves. The problem in this scenario is lack of respect for a team member that has resulted in a lack of team unity and focus.

Listing Inappropriate Behavior

Discriminatory behavior has occurred on and off the field, in overt and covert ways. A clear attempt is being made to sabotage Tom's performance. On the field, there are intentional attempts to ruin Tom's pass completion record by throwing poor passes to him. He has been called every derogatory and humiliating term for homosexual that exists. The team has ostracized him on and off the field.

Determining What Action To Take

Like most issues that involve discrimination, the problem is not the victim. It is the disrespectful behavior toward the victim. The bottom line is that the discriminatory behavior has to stop. The team needs to remain focused and work as a unit if they are to achieve their goals.

Considering Possible Reactions
• Tom decides to quit the team.
• Team members come to the coach to encourage him to remove Tom from the team roster.
• Tom is physically beaten and no one on the team will say who did it.
• Tom decides to stay on the team and expects the coach to support him.
• The discriminatory behavior continues but becomes more covert.

Setting Up a Meeting With the Athlete

The meeting could come about in one of several ways. Tom could come to the coach, the team could initiate a meeting, or the coach could set up a meeting with either Tom or the team. If the team is harassing Tom, it is unlikely they will also pursue official channels, as this would only draw attention to their behavior.

However, if the team thinks that the coach is sympathetic to their attitude toward Tom, they may try to get him involved.

There are a number of ways to handle the situation, depending on the severity of the problem and the individual personalities involved. Choosing to ignore the behavior will signal one of three things to the team: one, that the coach is uncomfortable dealing with the issue; two, silent approval of the discriminatory behavior; or three, that the coach is unaware of the problem. None of these will result in a desirable outcome. A leader who doesn't take a stand loses the respect of the players. If the team senses that the coach is too uncomfortable to deal with the problem, the team's power and control shift from the coach to the players.

The more quickly the coach reacts to the situation, the better. Once disrespectful behavior escalates and a pattern of behavior is established, making reparations and restoring respect become difficult. Not only might the team lose its best wide receiver, but it could lose its stability and health as a community, because the foundation of trust, respect, fairness, caring, and compassion among the team members would likely be affected.

Meeting With the Player[1]

The coach may want to begin by meeting with Tom to let him know that he is aware of the situation and that he values him as a member of the team. This lets Tom know that the coach respects him and that he does not condone the team's behavior. A player under this type of intense social pressure from his teammates may decide to quit the team. If the coach wants to prevent this from happening, he needs to deal with the situation. It is not necessary in this meeting to engage in a discussion of Tom's sexual preference. Unless Tom initiates a discussion, his privacy should be respected. He is not the problem.

Meeting With Other Team Members

How the coach proceeds from this point will depend on the personalities of the players and the particular dynamics of the situation. "Divide and conquer" can be effective when dealing with

---

[1] This scenario could easily have been included in Part III, since the discriminatory behavior is the problem and it is a team issue. However, since it is an individual that is affected by the team's behavior, it was included in this section. Some modifications of the template categories were made to accommodate the discussion.

destructive group behavior. Meeting with the team leaders and discussing the team's goals and the destructiveness of the team's behavior lets the players know that the coach plans to take a proactive stand. Coaches who let players know, through their actions, that their own sexuality is not threatened by the possibility of working with a homosexual player demonstrate strength as leaders and maintain control over the behavior of the players.

Meeting With The Team

If a discussion with the team leaders about respect for others does not produce a change in attitude, the behavior will most likely continue. It may become more covert. A team meeting emphasizing the team goals, the shared values of the team, and the expectations and rules for behavior might be the next step. This attempt to reestablish the focus of the team may not end the destructive behavior, but it may prevent it from escalating by letting the team know the coach is going to take a proactive stand.

The team should not be allowed to discuss Tom's sexual preference. Respecting someone means respecting their feelings and their privacy. Making them a topic of public debate or team discussion is inappropriate. Particularly with sexual preference, even players who don't want to be involved sometimes join in out of fear that they will be labeled homosexual, too. Although a team meeting may not solve the problem entirely, the coach, by being a strong role model and taking a stand, may help some players decide to treat Tom respectfully.

Depending on the success of refocusing the team as a group, the coach may need to identify those players who are most overt and influential and meet with them individually. It may be necessary to let them know that their status on the team could be affected by their behavior toward Tom. This bottom line will send the message that anyone who is not respectful of another team member is expendable.

Considering Important Points

In order for a team to be successful and to work as a cohesive unit, team members need to have respect for each other. Particularly during adolescence, keeping a team's attention and energy focused on a common goal is difficult, because young people are influenced by peer pressure and the need to conform. This is compounded by their preoccupation with sexuality, triggered by hormonal changes that have a powerful influence on their behavior. It is a challenge for a coach to build a positive community with a group of players from different backgrounds, cultures, religions, races, and sexual preferences. This challenge can be even greater when working with adolescents.

Commonality. Although coaches may have their own biases and feelings regarding homosexuality, if the alleged homosexual player is not attempting to solicit or influence other team members, the player's sexual preference is neither the coach's nor the team's business. Allowing players to make public judgments about teammates erodes the foundation of trust, caring, and camaraderie that is the foundation of the team's health as a community. Teammates need to focus on what they have in common rather than their differences. Players do not have to be best friends off the field, or condone each other's lifestyles. They do need to be respectful of each other and behave according to the shared values of the team.

Possibility of Change. It may be that the team is so homophobic that the coach believes he will be unable to change the players' attitudes or behavior. This creates a difficult dilemma. Does the coach do what is consistent with the shared values of the team, or does he decide not to take a stand because it's a losing battle? The coach who believes in his principles will be compelled to take a stand. Whether the issue is sexual preference, race, ethnic background, or religion, taking a stand against discrimination is vital to the health of society.

Community Goals. As noted by Gardner (1990), strong leaders look to the long-term goals of the community and act in ways that keep the vision, values, and goals of the group in focus. A coach may not change attitudes that took players years to develop, but taking a stand against discrimination will have an impact. It may be the only experience the players have that requires them to behave respectfully toward others and show respect for their differences.

Inclusive Environment. There are times and places for exclusive groups. However, public schools are designed to be inclusive. In our culturally diverse society, public school plays a unique role. It is the funnel through which we send our young people that shapes their identity as American citizens. Therefore, those who wish to participate in school and community based programs such as a sport team have chosen to be a part of an inclusive group. On the field, participants must focus on what they have in common, and behave in ways that are consistent with the shared values of the community.

Academic classrooms focus on students' cognitive development, and most of the interaction is between teacher and student. Athletics, physical education, band, and some other extracurricular activities provide opportunities for students to work with each other as a primary focus. Because of the diverse makeup of American society, we need to provide young people with educational experiences that allow them to learn about, work with, and respect others. Ignorance and fear are precursors to hatred and discrimination. Sport programs can provide structured educational opportunities for young people to work with individuals who are different from themselves. The nature of the experiences, however, is strongly influenced by the intentional community, its shared values, and the environment created under the coach's leadership.

Professional Conduct:
Personal Relationships With Players

Shuana, a ninth-grade softball player, has a crush on her male coach. She displays flirtatious behavior by giggling and making personal comments about the coach's anatomy and style of dress. She inappropriately competes with other team members for his attention. The team is aware of her crush and is acutely sensitive to the player-coach interactions during practice. This behavior is affecting the team's concentration and focus.

Analyzing the Issue

Identifying the Problem

The player's behavior is affecting team unity and cohesiveness. It is a distraction for both players and coach. The atmosphere at practices is not focused on the team activities but on the interaction between the coach and one player. At this point, it is only a behavior problem, but it could easily escalate into an ethical issue, a criminal act, or a civil violation (Title IX), depending on how the coach handles the situation.

Listing Inappropriate Behavior
- Player makes inappropriate comments or gestures regarding the coach.
- She publicly comments on the coach's anatomy and dress. The comments are flirtatious and clearly intended to embarrass the coach.
- She giggles during the coach's demonstrations and explanations.
- She asks questions and tries to get special attention and treatment.
- She attempts to spend one-on-one time with the coach.

Determining What Action To Take
The purpose of meeting with this athlete is to identify the inappropriate behaviors that must stop. This means that the coach must describe specific comments and incidents that have occurred, such as the comment about his legs or giggling during a skill demonstration. Once the behavior has been identified, the coach should refocus the athlete on the team goals, indicate her value as a player and team member, and then explain the boundaries and nature of all coach/player relationships. Depending on the response of the athlete, the coach can either use the meeting as an educational session without a specific warning, or give a specific consequence if it should happen again.

Considering Possible Reactions by the Athlete
- Player denies any special feelings beyond coach/player relationship.
- Player exploits the situation and openly expresses her feelings.
- Player is embarrassed and uncomfortable with the discussion and withdraws.
- Player becomes humiliated and emotional.
- Player becomes angry and takes the coach's boundaries as a personal rejection.
- Player accuses the coach of flirting with her.

Setting Up a Meeting With the Athlete

The coach should arrange the meeting at the end of practice and hold it immediately to prevent the player from misinterpreting its purpose. The coach should have a third party present (teacher or administrator) or meet somewhere in full view of others (such as in the bleachers of the gymnasium when others are present,) although the actual conversation may be private. If held privately in an office, the door should be open with a desk between the coach and player.

Outlining the Meeting

Opening the Meeting and Presenting the Problem

The coach's demeanor should be businesslike, with a firm but compassionate manner. He should outline the reason for the meeting by indicating the inappropriate behaviors the athlete has demonstrated in the last few practices. Examples need to be brought to Shuana's attention. Any inappropriate behavior that occurs during the meeting should be confronted immediately. For example, if an overly aggressive athlete suggests getting together over the weekend, the coach can use this as an example, followed with an explanation of the reasons.

Taking Action

It is not necessary to label Shuana's behavior as a crush or a romantic interest, as long as the inappropriate behavior is clearly understood by the athlete. The coach can let her know that he values her as a player on the team, but that the relationship must remain a professional one. The coach may need to define the boundaries of the coach/player relationship and the need for fairness to all players. This allows him to maintain a firm bottom line, but it may minimize the impact of the message as a personal rejection. It also helps the player learn the appropriate boundaries for professional relationships.

Closing the Meeting

The coach can summarize the meeting by emphasizing the specific positive contributions Shuana makes to the team as a player. Unless she has resisted the boundaries the coach has outlined during the meeting, he can end positively by letting her know that he is confident she can make the behavioral adjustments. If Shuana has been resistant to the coach's boundaries, he may need to include the consequences for future inappropriate behavior.

Considering Important Points

Coaches who are hired (or volunteer) to coach youth or school athletic teams are entrusted with the well-being of their athletes. Theirs is a professional duty to safeguard the physical and emotional health of their players. As leaders, coaches also have a responsibility to treat team members fairly and to use their power and authority appropriately. Even when players are consenting adults, the power and authority that coaches have over their players make a sexual relationship at best inadvisable and at worst an abuse of this authority. Of course, when players are underage (defined by state statute) a sexual relationship is illegal.

Respect. Team participation is a social experience that provides players with opportunities to learn about relationships with others. Through the expectations they create, coaches have tremendous influence on the way players behave toward their teammates, opponents, officials, coaches, spectators, and even their own young admirers. For example, players learn fairly quickly that game officials cannot be addressed with the same candor or informality that is generally acceptable with their teammates. They also learn to shake hands with opposing team members after a game as a way of showing respect for their opponents and the game.

Boundaries. One of the responsibilities of the coach is to help players understand the boundaries of the various types of relationships that exist in the sport environment. One way, coaches teach their players how to behave toward others is by modeling the behavior they expect. When the nature of a coach's relationship with a player changes from professional to personal, the boundaries for behavior become blurred for everyone—coach, players, and team. It also affects the players' sense of fairness and their respect for relationship boundaries. Because of the inherent inequities of power and authority between coaches and players, a coach needs to question his or her motives concerning a relationship with a player.

Intensity. Given the amount of time players and coaches spend together and the intensity of the competitive athletic environment, it is not surprising that emotional ties and feelings develop among the participants. It is normal and common for players to develop crushes on their coach. It is also not surprising that coaches develop feelings for their players (Kirby, Greaves, & Hankivsky, 2000; Wahl, Wertheim, & Dohmann, 2001). However, as the adult and authority figure, a coach who acts on these feelings jeopardizes and often compromises the best interests of the player and the team.

Coach-Player Relationship. As will be discussed in greater detail in the chapter on sexual harassment (Chapter 9), NASPE has taken a strong and definitive stand against any type of romantic relationship between coach and player. This position is echoed by the United States Olympic Committee in their Coaching Ethics Code (U.S. Olympic Committee, 2003), which states that coaches should not have "sexual intimacies" with current or former athletes. Although it discourages any sexual relationship with former athletes, the USOC recommends a minimum of two years between the end of the coaching relationship and any sexual intimacies. Although many sports organizations do not have explicit policies governing coach-player relationships (Wahl et al., 2001, p. 70), coaches who are paid employees of school districts are usually held to the standards of personal conduct for teachers. In most jurisdictions, teacher-student sexual relationships are prohibited.

It may be helpful for coaches to know that players with crushes are not usually romantically interested in them. Although flirtatious behavior may be overtly sexual in nature, its intent is often to make the player feel special to the coach, rather than a signal of sexual interest. This understanding can make it easier for a coach to deal with an athlete's behavior and feelings. This does not, however, minimize the inappropriateness of the behavior, whether it is a sophisticated overture or an immature attempt at flirting.

Sexual Harassment. Sexual harassment claims are a concern for anyone in a position of power and authority. Although they may not be grounded in fact, any student or athlete can make a sexual harassment claim. An athlete who feels rejected by a coach can seek retribution by making a false claim. Unfortunately, unless there are witnesses, the allegations, true or not, can wreak havoc on a coach's career. Coaches need to keep their antennae up and avoid spending time alone with players, particularly when there is any cause for concern. Documenting player behavior and the actions taken by the coach can be very helpful. Making colleagues and an immediate supervisor aware of the issue from its onset is also important. Any adult-witnessed interactions with the player are very helpful if it is necessary to have corroborating evidence for an account of what happened.

A coach who gives differential or special treatment to any player is vulnerable to claims of harassment and/or statutory rape if the player is underage. At the very least, the coach can be accused of unprofessional behavior and favoritism or bias. Once athletes perceive the coach as "available," the nature of the interactions between players and the coach may take on a social agenda. As a result of either inaccurate information or rumors, there can be compounding effects on the team as well as the individual athlete involved with the coach.

It is important in all such issues to identify the problematic behavior and assess the severity of the situation, but this problem is sometimes more difficult because it involves the coach on a personal level. Misidentifying, mishandling, or under- or overestimating the situation can have severe consequences for the coach, player, and team. It can be misjudged for a number of reasons. The age, sex, maturity level, and emotional stability of the player as well as an honest assessment of the coach's feelings toward the athlete are all factors that must be carefully taken into consideration before deciding how to deal with the problem.

If the player is an assertive and mature individual with whom the coach would otherwise consider having a relationship, the coach needs to be very careful. Extra care must be taken not to show differential treatment to this player. Maintaining a professional relationship and avoiding all situations that could result in being alone with the player are essential. Handling personal overtures from a player under this circumstance is often more difficult than when the child is younger and less mature. Even if the coach handles the situation directly and lets the player know that a relationship is not acceptable, the possibility that the rejection could result in an untrue accusation should be considered. With this in the back of their minds, many coaches do not spend time alone with their athletes.

SCENARIO 8

Respect for Opponents:
Intent To Injure

John is the starting sweeper on the soccer team. He is a very aggressive player. In the last two games, he fouled the opposing team's top-scoring players. Both of these players were injured seriously and most likely sidelined for the rest of the season. The coach's review of what has happened leads him to believe that John's motive was to take the opposing players out of the game rather than to play the ball. His aggressive behavior has consistently targeted the opposing team's highest-scoring players and has occurred when the team is losing. The coach let John know that he does not condone dangerous play or an intent to injure an opponent. However, as the last line of defense in front of the goal, the coach has also let him know what the expectation is for the starting sweeper: to stop opponents from scoring.

Analyzing the Issue

Identifying the Problem

John's pattern of behavior suggests that he is willing to do whatever it takes to prevent the opposing team from scoring goals and winning the game. Specifically, it does not look like he is attempting to play the ball. The way fouls have occurred, it looks as though he was attempting to intentionally injure the players. These fouls consistently have occurred against key players in tight game situations.

Listing Inappropriate Behavior

If John is attempting to play the player first and the ball second it is inappropriate. Boys' soccer is considered a contact sport. However, contact must be the result of an attempt to play the ball. Furthermore, John has shown no concern for the injuries he has caused as a result of his fouls.

Determining What Action To Take

The coach needs to examine the facts and circumstances that have led to the injuries of the opposing players. If, in the coach's

opinion, John has intentionally tried to take the players out of the game, and if the coach wants to prevent it from happening again, he may have to make the consequences for another occurrence very severe. This could include suspension or removal from the team.

In the event that John denies intent to harm the opposing players, and if the coach wants to stop the aggressive behavior, it may be necessary to let John know that if he causes another injury he will be suspended. This may seem to be an extreme measure, but it may be necessary, because making a judgment about intent is very difficult, particularly in a game that is as physical as boys' soccer.

However, if game outcomes are more important to the coach than the physical well-being of the participants, then it will be difficult for the coach to follow through with suspension or removal from the team as a consequence. Giving John the benefit of the doubt when making a judgment about his intent to cause harm and allowing him to continue playing with a verbal reprimand would be a more likely action. This would allow the coach to continue playing John.

Considering Possible Reactions by the Athlete
- Player denies the intent to cause harm and rationalizes that the increased aggression was a result of an "adrenaline rush" in tough game situations.
- Player admits that the game was very physical but that he was only defending himself against the aggressive behavior of his opponents.
- Player admits his intent to injure opposing players.

Setting Up a Meeting With the Athlete

One way to communicate the gravity of the problem to John is to formalize the meeting in the coach's office. The coach may want to have some discussion with John regarding his perception of the incidents and their circumstances. However, if the coach wants to stop the overly aggressive behavior, he will keep the meeting focused on what is appropriate and inappropriate behavior and the consequences of a repeat occurrence. This probably will be a short- to medium-length meeting.

Outlining the Meeting

Opening the Meeting and Presenting the Problem
If the coach has set a serious tone for the meeting, then it is likely that John knows the coach is unhappy with something he has done. With this as a backdrop, the coach may want to open the meeting by letting John know that he is a valuable team member. He can then turn to the reason for the meeting and the seriousness of the issue. It is critical to the long-term coach-player relationship to focus on John's behavior rather than on him as a person.

As with most behavior issues, the more specifically the coach can define what is appropriate and inappropriate, the better the chances of the athlete changing his behavior and of keeping the player-coach relationship positive. In this case, the rules of the game and the referees are independent sources of feedback for the player. If John has received fouls for his aggressive behavior, for example, this can validate the coach's interpretation of the situation.

Intent to harm is another issue. Although officials may immediately eject or "red card" a player for blatantly aggressive behavior like fighting or swearing, if the behavior is not obvious, they generally will not make a judgment about "intent." This judgment is one the coach may have to make alone. One of the important signals the coach should pay attention to is whether the player has any remorse for the injuries he has caused. Regardless of intent, if the player has no remorse for what has happened, this may be a sign of more serious problems, and may be beyond the coach's influence.

It is important that the coach clearly outline what behavior is appropriate and inappropriate. If he has game tapes, reviewing them with John would be an effective way of making sure that he knows when his behavior became inappropriate. In the absence of video tapes, the coach needs to define clearly the gray area between assertive play and overly aggressive behavior in terms that are as observable as possible. This lets the player know the criteria on which the coach is making the decision about his future with the team. Once John understands the line between inappropriate and appropriate behavior, he can better control his playing destiny.

Taking Action

The coach needs to be sure that John understands that his behavior is not acceptable. He needs to be given clear-cut consequences for another incident.

Closing the Meeting

Once the issue has been defined, discussed, and understood, John needs to know the consequences of future occurrences as well as any repercussions for what has already occurred. Ending the meeting on a positive and optimistic note will help maintain a positive relationship. If John understands appropriate and inappropriate behavior, but cannot control his behavior, then suspension from the team and referral to counseling will probably be necessary.

Considering Important Points

Aggression and Anger. There are many who believe that sport can be used as an outlet for aggression—that it purges pent-up feelings of anger and hostility. According to this belief, once aggressive feelings have been channeled through sport as an "appropriate" outlet, individuals can return to "real life" purged of anger and frustration and in control of their behavior. The analogy is made to the pressure building inside a volcano; once it is released, the situation returns to a calm and nonagitated state. A 1995 study by Russell, Arms, and Bibby, found that 63 percent of people polled held this belief. However, research findings do not sup-

port the theory that sport has a cathartic effect (Dunnings, 1999; Phillips, 1983; Sipes, 1975, 1996). If not for its cathartic value, why are aggressive and violent behaviors so prevalent in male sports in particular?

A number of factors seem to play a role in the acceptance of aggression prevalent in male contact sports.[1] Sociologists have theorized that sport violence among male athletes is linked to their gender ideology. Male athletes are socialized to accept aggressive and even violent behavior as part of the game. The criteria for evaluation of contact sport athletes is often the ability to take a pounding, to play in spite of injuries, and to have the toughness to give it back. In many sports, use of intimidation, aggression, and violence are seen as a legitimate part of game strategy. Also termed the "sport ethic," this norm creates powerful expectations for behavior and is intimately linked with players' masculine identity (Coakley, 2001).

---

[1] For a more in-depth overview of aggression and violence in sport, see Jay Coakley (2001), *Sport in Society, Issues and Controversy*. Coakley defines aggression as "verbal or physical behavior grounded in an intent to dominate, control, or do harm to another person" (p. 175). He defines violence as "the use of excessive physical force, which causes or has the potential to cause harm or destruction" (p. 174).

Acceptable Behavior. Coaches who do not want to perpetuate this "sport ethic" may be challenged for several reasons. First, coaches who played the sport more than likely experienced and accepted these expectations for their behavior. It is likely that their own masculine identity was shaped by these experiences. Second, a lack of social support in the team environment—fans, officials, parents, other coaches, and even the players themselves—make change a formidable task. However, coaches can create rules and expectations for players that draw a definitive line between acceptable and unacceptable behavior. Coaches who consistently remove overly aggressive players from the game can influence the behavior of their players in the game.

Physical Contact. Research on male contact sports indicates that as the degree of physical contact in a sport increases, so does the acceptance of some types of aggressive behaviors (Bredemeier & Shields, 1985, 1986; White & Young, 1997). The sociologist Mike Messner (1992) suggests that the masculinity of boys and men who play sports that are high in physical contact are evaluated in part by their aggressiveness. Messner also reports that most male power and performance sport athletes view aggressive acts as a legitimate part of the game as long as they are within the rule structure of the game and consistent with the informal criteria players use to evaluate each other.

According to research by Weinstein, Smith, and Wiesenthal (1995), young male athletes learn that they are evaluated by coaches, peers, and the community based on their ability to commit aggressive and violent acts on the field. Once players figure out that aggressive and violent behaviors are criteria for getting playing time, it isn't surprising that these behaviors escalate in frequency and intensity. When players receive more playing time or are elevated in status on the team for actions that are overly aggressive or violent, they are rewarded for the behavior. Further, if this behavior is associated with increased masculinity, boys and young men may be even more encouraged to engage in this behavior.

Clear Guidance. In the scenario with John, the coach had let him know that, as the last line of defense, it was really important that he prevent shots on their goal. Although the coach never overtly endorsed intentionally hurting another player, the message John received was ambiguous and certainly open to interpretation.

He may have felt he was pleasing the coach by taking the players who were the biggest threat out of the game.

Reasonable Restraint. In addition to powerful cultural influences, there are some developmental factors that have implications for those coaching school-age athletes. It is the ability to reason that can prevent humans from engaging in behaviors that are maladaptive and contrary to moral or legal codes. According to Daniel Weinberger, director of Clinical Brain Disorders Laboratory at the National Institute of Health (2001), the prefrontal cortex is the area of the brain that enables humans to reason and exercise restraint and self-control in situations when the overwhelming urge is to do the opposite. The prefrontal cortex of the brain is not fully formed until about the age of 20. A more recent review of the research on brain development (Strauch, 2003) suggests that the brain may not be fully developed till age 25. This means that the adolescent reasoning center of the brain is biologically immature. Young people confronted with difficult decisions in intensely competitive situations that threaten their ego or their standing in a community may not be developmentally capable of reacting reasonably or with restraint.

Supervised Decision-Making. Thus, it is important that young people have the guidance and supervision of adults to help them maintain control, particularly in stressful situations that require quick decision-making. In highly competitive and physical situations common in sport, any individuals, but particularly those more prone to violent behavior, may be more likely to commit aggressive acts that could have life-altering consequences. Given this developmental characteristic, it is important that coaches, officials, and parents work together to help young people learn to reason and exercise self-control. Players need to have experiences that require them to make choices in difficult situations, in supervised environments that will allow them to develop this ability safely. It may even be necessary for adults to step in and make decisions for players in situations that are developmentally beyond their abilities.

Aggression Versus Skill. It is also commonly believed that aggressive behavior can offset skill, conditioning, and strategic limitations. That is, a team can make up for their lack of skill or conditioning by playing more aggressively. In fact, a study of professional hockey teams (Engelhardt, 1995) has found the opposite trend. In a study of National Hockey League hockey teams and league standings, the teams with the most fouls for violent behavior were not the teams with the best win-loss records. In Engelhardt's study, the teams with the best win-loss records had the fewest fouls for aggressive play. Although more research is needed, the idea that more aggressive teams win more is not necessarily true.

Life Skills. While the model of professional sport and its economic realities are ever present in our lives, it is important to keep in mind the role that sport plays in our society for young people. It can provide them with experiences that allow them to exercise those behaviors that will be necessary to succeed in a competitive society. Self-control, goal-orientation, tenacity, a strong work ethic, and the ability to work with others are all desirable traits. However, one does not need to win the league championship to develop these traits or learn from these experiences. In fact, since most competitions only have one winner, learning to bounce back from losing, to maintain self-control under pressure, and to stay focused and motivated under adversity are skills that may be used far more in life than learning to win graciously.

Pregame Pep Talks. Coaches who use pregame team pep talks and psychological motivators, such as ritualistic chanting, to psyche players up for a game may actually be doing more harm than good. Although their purpose may be to increase players' arousal level and make players more competitive, assertive, or aggressive, these motivational techniques may not produce the desired result. Research on arousal and athletic performance provide no magic formula for coaches who want their players optimally aroused on game day. Research suggests that arousal is a multidimensional and complex construct that involves the mind, body, and emotions (Zaichkowsky & Baltzell, 2001).

Individual Techniques. Coaches who use the same motivational techniques for an entire team may be over-arousing some players and under-arousing others. In addition, if raising arousal levels increases anxiety, athletes who do not perform well may have a more difficult time recovering from the disappointment. Players who are over-aroused before an adrenaline-producing team pep talk may actually need to be relaxed or focused prior to the game.

In addition to individual differences, factors that have been found to influence arousal and performance are task complexity, skill level of the performer, attentional processes, and player's appraisal and outlook for the outcome of the competitive situation (Zaichkowsky & Baltzell, 2001).

Limits. Coaches who want to limit aggressive behavior should set definite boundaries for player behavior on and off the field. Equally important is the model the coach sets for his or her players. Coaches who act aggressively are often seen and not heard. Coaches who verbally or physically abuse players encourage their players to behave the same way toward others. On the other hand, coaches who show compassion and empathy are more likely to bring out those behaviors in their athletes. A positive role model is essential for players to develop self-control and respect for the health and safety of others. Coaches who value winning more than the well-being of others will telegraph that message through their actions.

Teachable Moments. In addition to being a good role model, taking advantage of teachable moments is also important. Pointing out a player who has exercised self-control in a difficult situation and letting the team know that, as a coach, you are proud of that player's behavior sends a clear message. It is also important when discussing difficult situations and issues with players to focus on the reasons for the decisions. Working through decision-making processes with players and sharing the reasons for decisions with players helps them learn how to identify the values underlying their own decisions and behavior.

Discussion

Prior to the 1990s, incidents of violence in youth and school sports were rarely adjudicated in courts of law. Acts of aggression were handled by officials and, in more severe instances, by league administrators. Depending on the severity of the acts, the sanctions were either suspension from games or expulsion from a team or league. However, in the past decade, violence has not been effectively controlled by the rules and sanctions of the game. Serious injuries and deaths have occurred as a result of out-of-control players, coaches, officials, fans, and parents. Many of these incidents have resulted in criminal charges and incarceration.

PART III

Issues Involving the Team as a Community
Leadership Decisions, Actions, and the Messages They Send

INTRODUCTION

In addition to the common coaching problems discussed in Part II that focused on individual players, there are also problems that are not specific to an individual, but are team concerns. The use of performance-enhancing supplements, parental and spectator behavior, initiation rites, hazing, and sexual harassment are team issues that can have a strong influence on the educational experience of sport participants. Part III discusses these topics and provides knowledge, insight, and ideas for coaches who want to make players' experiences as nurturing and positive as possible.

CHAPTER 6

Performance-Enhancing Supplements

Raoul, a high school freshman, was a well-liked, easy-going guy. He was popular, bright, and a talented athlete. Concerned about his playing time because he was a little on the small side for football, Raoul joined Royd's gym at the suggestion of his coach. It was commonly known in the athletic community that if you worked out at Royd's gym, you could get anabolic steroids to make your efforts more worthwhile.

Raoul became a regular at the gym, and with the help of anabolic steroids he gained 30 pounds of muscle during his freshman year. At the beginning of the following season, Coach Johnson took notice of the dramatic changes in Raoul's physique and complimented him on his dedication and hard work. He suggested to some of the other players that they talk to Raoul and follow his program.

There were also other changes in Raoul, however. He was aggressive on the field and had developed a very quick temper—on and off the field. He had developed enlarged breasts, commonly referred to as "bitch teats." Tony, one of his teammates, sarcastically asked him what size bra he wore. No longer the easy-going guy that he had been, Raoul slammed Tony into a locker and punched him in the face, breaking his jaw. Tony and his parents filed criminal and civil charges and Raoul was arrested for assault.

Discussion

It is probable that Raoul is a victim of "roid rage." Increased aggression is a side effect of anabolic steroid use that has been widely reported. This scenario raises a number of issues for coaches to think about.

It is not clear whether Coach Johnson knew that Raoul was taking anabolic steroids. Given the prevalence of steroid use in sports and the dramatic changes in Raoul's size and strength, it was a likely possibility. These signs, along with the gym's reputation, were reasons to question Raoul's physical transformation. Perhaps Coach Johnson did not want to know. It is also possible that he suggested Raoul go to that particular gym knowing he would be introduced to performance-enhancing supplements.

Does the coach have an obligation to try to influence players' behavior when they are on their own time? Assuming Coach Johnson did not explicitly encourage Raoul to take steroids, does that absolve him of culpability? What are the possible motives of a coach who encourages players to take steroids or herbal supplements? Because of the established health risks, which will be discussed in the next section, this is not a right-versus-right dilemma. When coaches choose not to take proactive action to prevent players from taking dangerous drugs, they are breaching their professional, moral, and perhaps legal obligation to protect their players' welfare. The most important responsibility of coaches in youth and school sports is the health and safety of their athletes.

It is natural in competitive situations to do everything possible to gain a competitive edge. It isn't surprising that players are tempted to use performance-enhancing drugs to give them that edge. Most competitive organizations have taken a strong stand against drugs such as anabolic steroids. Many have established expensive and elaborate drug-testing programs to discourage their use. Because of the expense and administrative difficulties, most youth and high school sport programs generally do not have drug-testing programs. This leaves the primary responsibility for preventing their use to the sport coaches.

The obvious motivation of a coach who allows players to take performance-enhancing supplements is to win. Coaches who do not explicitly take a stand against such drugs give players silent permission to do what it takes to improve themselves. Educating players about the health risks associated with steroid use is the best preventive measure a coach can take.

When presenting information to athletes, it is important to give a thorough and balanced picture of the benefits and health hazards of steroid use. Players who believe they are not being given all the facts often choose not to take any of the information seriously. Discussions, a video, or a talk from someone in the community who has a personal story can have a profound influence on players. Players with self-respect and self-esteem are better equipped to resist the short-term benefits of anabolic steroids.

What Are Anabolic Steroids?

Androgenic anabolic steroids (AS) are synthetic forms of the male hormone testosterone. Steroids are a class of drugs legally available only by prescription. Anabolic means "building," and anabolic steroids promote the growth of skeletal muscle, increase lean body mass, and promote the development of male sex characteristics. Concerns about athletic performance and body image have led to an increase in the use of anabolic steroids in both male and female teens and adults despite their serious side effects and health consequences.

How Prevalent Is the Use of Anabolic Steroids?

A longitudinal study by the National Institute on Drug Abuse (NIDA, 2000) of steroid use among middle and high school students indicated that steroid use is on the rise. Although more males are using steroids than females, steroid use is growing fastest among females. The study also found that 12th-grade students had a decreased perceived risk of harm from steroid use than had been found in previous groups of 12th graders. Research studies of the prevalence of AS have reported between 3 and 11 percent of high school boys and up to 2 percent of high school girls have used steroids (NIDA, 2000). Although not examined in these studies, it would be interesting to know what percentage of these users were athletes.

Use of AS has been found across a wide variety of sports, from bodybuilding and football to track and field and baseball. In addition to the size and strength gains, steroids are beneficial to power and endurance athletes because they enable them to train more frequently at higher intensities and to extend the duration of their workouts. Steroids can also decrease recovery time necessary between workouts (Yesalis & Cowart, 1998).

What Are the Health Hazards of AS Use?

In addition to educating players and taking a strong stand, coaches need to be aware of the typical signs, symptoms, and side effects of anabolic steroid use. In males and females the side effects of AS abuse can include:

- Cardiovascular disease, the long-term effects of which are not fully known. Because AS use has been found to increase blood pressure and affect cholesterol levels by increasing the LDL (bad cholesterol) and decreasing the HDL (good cholesterol), it is thought that it can lead to heart attacks and strokes.
- Liver tumors and cancer.
- Jaundice (which is yellowish pigmentation of skin, body fluids, and tissue).
- Severe acne.
- Water retention—particularly in the neck and facial areas.
- Trembling.

Sex-Related Side Effects

In females, side effects can include the development of male sex characteristics such as growth of facial hair, male-pattern baldness, deepened voice, enlargement of the clitoris, breast tissue atrophy, cessation of the menstrual cycle, and an increase in sex drive. Some of these effects are thought to be irreversible.

Sex-specific side effects for males can include shrinking testicles, reduced sperm count, infertility, baldness, increased risk for prostate cancer, and development of breasts. When males take high doses of AS over time, the body shuts down its own production of testosterone. It also can convert excessive amounts of male hormone to estrogen, a female hormone. This can result in the development of breasts (clinically termed gynecomastia), often referred to by steroid users as "bitch teats." This effect has been found to be irreversible.

Psychological Side Effects of AS

In addition to physical side effects, there is evidence to suggest that there are also psychological side effects. These are particularly likely when the doses of AS are high. Aggression, also known as "roid rages," can range from extreme mood swings, depression, and irritability to manic-like episodes that often lead to violence. Sexual desire is known to be dependent on the male hormone testosterone, as is aggressiveness. Other psychological side effects include sleep disorders, euphoria, confusion, pathological anxiety, paranoia, and hallucinations.

It is difficult to establish the precise behavioral effects of AS use for a number of reasons. First, there are literally hundreds of different anabolic steroids. Second, it is illegal to prescribe AS to enhance athletic performance. Therefore, athletes must obtain their supply through the black market. This makes monitoring the quality, dosages, and effects of the drugs difficult. Third, individual athlete reactions to identical dosages of the same drug can vary widely. Fourth, some athletes use multiple performance-enhancing substances concurrently.

We do know that testosterone production in both males and females (females have testosterone, too) is controlled by the hypothalamus, a group of nerve cells at the base of the brain. The hypothalamus also controls appetite, blood pressure, reproductive ability, and moods, including feelings of depression, irritability, and aggression. It is likely that AS use alters the body's hormonal balance and has widespread physical and psychological effects. These effects are probably even more critical during adolescence, when the body is already experiencing dramatic hormonal changes.

Unique Risk to Young AS Users

For young athletes who have not finished growing, AS use appears to cause premature closing of the bone growth plates. Once the plates have closed, no further bone growth may occur. This means that for AS users who have not attained their full height, their growth will be stunted.

Availability and Method of Use of AS

Another factor that influences the effects of AS is the method of use. Steroids are usually taken either orally or by injection. The oral method of use has been found to have more negative side effects than intramuscular injections. Cycling or alternating periods of usage; stacking, using several different types of AS concurrently; and pyramiding, progressively and systematically increasing then decreasing doses through a specified time period, are all ways of maximizing benefits and minimizing detrimental effects. There are a wide variety of resources on the Internet for those who want to learn about the use of steroids and their performance-enhancing effects.

Herbal and Dietary Supplements

Some athletes who want to take performance-enhancing drugs, but do not want to get them through the black market, may choose dietary or herbal supplements as an alternative. Because these supplements are legal and readily available without a medical prescription, they are often thought to be safe. Because herbal and dietary supplements are not legally considered "drugs," they are not subject to the research and testing scrutiny of the FDA.

This does not mean that they do not have side effects or risks. It only means that there is no legally mandated control over their use. In fact, if dietary and herbal supplements achieve performance-enhancing outcomes similar to AS, it is likely that they react similarly in the body. The side effects would be similar also. Players who choose this alternative may not be doing anything illegal, but that does not mean that there are fewer physical or psychological health risks. It only means that the risks are unknown.

Ephedra, a dietary supplement that claims to boost energy and spur weight loss is an example of a performance-enhancing dietary supplement used by athletes. Ephedra is also known as ephedrine, the Chinese herb ma huang, and was contained in a popular athletic performance booster called Ripped Fuel. Although legal to buy in a health food store, like other herbal and dietary supplements, its effects on the body were largely unknown. It became a popular supplement for professional athletes, student athletes, and adolescents. Because there was no legally mandated advance testing for ephedra containing supplements, serious health concerns were not noticed until its use became fairly widespread. High blood pressure, racing heart rates, strokes, seizures, and deaths were among the problems reported by subsequent research studies.

The FDA has reported more than 80 deaths and 1,000 adverse reactions from its use. In a study of ephedrine use published in *The New England Journal of Medicine,* Haller and Benowitz (2000) found that of the 140 adverse reactions reported, nearly all of the cases were—more than likely—linked to the use of ephedrine.

Despite the mounting evidence of problems with ephedra, the dietary supplement industry has strongly protested regulatory control of its products and has defended the use of products such as ephedra. However, the National Football League and the NCAA have banned the use of ephedra. The problems with ephedra are typical of all dietary supplements. There are no controls for the actual content of the substances as claimed on the packaging, all ingredients and dosages are not checked for accuracy, and no advance testing is done to verify the purported benefits or liabilities of the products prior to their sale.

Signs for Coaches to Look For

There are signs a coach can look for that signal AS (or other supplement) use. The obvious signs are quick weight and strength gains. However, strength gains will only occur when AS are taken in conjunction with a weight-training program. Swelling in the face, neck, feet, and lower legs from water retention, trembling, purple or red spots on the body or unexplained darkening of the skin, jaundice, and a persistent unpleasant breath odor are signs of possible use. Irritability, combativeness, and aggressiveness are also signs of use.

Summary

Whether the motivation is to gain an advantage, to win, or just look better, the short-term benefits of AS are not without established long-term health consequences. Coaches who do not take a proactive stand and educate their players about both AS and herbal supplements may be perceived by their players as giving them "silent endorsement." Although illegal to prescribe for its use in sport, AS are readily available through the black market, at some gyms, and on the Internet.

Herbal supplements are not illegal and can be obtained at health-food stores and on the Internet. The problem with herbal supplements is that there is no quality control or dosage information about these substances. Compounding these problems is a lack of well-controlled research studies on their short- and long-term health effects.

Coaches need to be aware of the prevalence of AS use. Young people who generally are not part of the "drug" or "alcohol" scene can be lured into using supplements in order to help them achieve their goals. Educating athletes at the youth sports level about the health risks associated with such supplements is a good preventive measure. Coaches who let players and parents know about both the short-term benefits and the long-term health risks of performance supplements give players the knowledge they need to resist temptation. Coaches can also steer players away from workout facilities where they are more likely to be introduced to these substances.

Coaches are not directly responsible for what players do on their own time. However, because players are often eager to meet the expectations of their coaches, using this influence to help players think about their long-term best interests can be pivotal. Educating players and taking a stand will encourage them to make the right decision.

CHAPTER 7

Beyond the Immediate Community: Working With Parents and Spectators

Johnny, who plays second singles as a sophomore on your tennis team, has not been playing well. His father comes to all the matches and "coaches" him from courtside. He is very critical of any mistakes Johnny makes and his comments are made with brutal sarcasm for all to hear. He also makes comments about Johnny's opponents. The coach can see that Johnny loses his concentration and is embarrassed by his father's behavior. Some parents and spectators are annoyed, while others have begun making comments, too.

Inappropriate Spectator Behavior

Parents, or any spectators, should not make public comments to anyone—an official, coach, player, or another spectator. This includes their own children. Parents are not a part of the coaching staff. When players are taking part in team activities, they are under the

supervision of the coach. Interruptions, comments, or distractions of any kind by parents or spectators, regardless of intent, are inappropriate. This includes judgmental comments about coaching, officiating, or player behavior. Even well-intentioned positive coaching from the sidelines can be inappropriate.

Dealing With Spectators

It is difficult to deal with spectators after a negative public display has escalated to the point where it is out of control. Because spectators are not part of the team, coaches do not have formal jurisdiction over their behavior. However, in most sports that have officials, there are rules officials can invoke that involve spectator behavior, which may be helpful with unruly spectators. A coach who anticipates problems can alert officials to potential difficulties before the game starts. Officials can then take immediate action when situations arise and help the coach keep spectators under control. If the coach, school, or league has additional established guidelines and rules for spectator behavior, then dealing with people who are not following them can be fairly straightforward. If the guidelines include consequences for noncompliance, then the coach needs to be sure to apply them consistently.

If there are no established guidelines, one option is to interrupt the game or match and make a formal announcement asking the spectators for their cooperation. Asking the fans to refrain from commenting so players can stay focused lets the spectators know what the expectations are for their behavior. Of course, making the announcement in a controlled and respectful way is important, since that is the behavior the coach wants the parents and spectators to demonstrate.

There are several possible reactions to such an announcement. Spectators may not listen or may make disruptive comments. Or, they may listen, but continue the behavior after the announcement. Generally, most people will comply, but there is often a small percentage of people who continue to be disruptive.

If possible, it is helpful to get the names of the people who are most disruptive. Generally, it is not effective to speak with them about their behavior publicly or when they are having difficulty with self-control. This could escalate the situation. Also, in order to preserve their dignity, discussions with individual spectators should take place privately. If the coach is afraid for his or her own safety, then speaking to the individual in a public place where others are present, but out of hearing range, can be a good alternative.

Meeting With the Parents

Some coaches hold a mandatory meeting for parents at the beginning of the season. Although parents are not team members, they need to understand and accept the goals, rules, and expectations of the team. Some parents will want to know about winning and how playing time is determined. The coach should be prepared to discuss how competitive the program is, the method of selecting starting players, how playing time is determined, practice attendance policies, goals, expectations, rules, and consequences for noncompliance.

Parents are a part of the extended community, and their cooperation and support are important. This meeting will set the tone for the relationship between the parents and the coach. The parameters for spectator and parental behavior should be outlined, and written team rules given to all parents to sign. If possible, having a league official or school administrator at the meeting is also a good idea. If there are to be consequences for noncompliance, it is best to have the endorsement of those who have the power to overrule your decision.

One preventive measure to control parental behavior was developed by a youth soccer league in Florida (Zarella, 2000). Two thousand parents were required to attend an ethics class and sign a contract that specified acceptable behavior at their children's games. Sanctions for noncompliance ranged from ejection from the game to lifetime suspension from the organization's sports programs. In some leagues, coaches and officials also sign codes of ethics for their behavior. Other organizations have dealt with the problem by establishing rules such as spectators must be silent during games or by banning adults from attendance at games.

Discussion

Coaches need to have a plan for handling disruptive situations that get out of control. When there is a threat of physical harm to anyone—players, spectators, officials, or coaches—more drastic measures, such as suspending the game, may be necessary. However, suspending a game for rude or unsportsperson-like conduct is a political decision that needs to be discussed with officials, the other coach, and district or league administrators. Coaches do not usually have the authority to make this decision unilaterally. Discussions of options with district personnel or league officials before problems arise make the decision-making process easier—particularly in difficult or unexpected situations.

Violent Behavior

Out-of-control parental behavior is escalating in youth and high school sports. Parental misconduct has gone far beyond verbally abusing an official. It has escalated to physical violence that has ended in death. Parental behavior in sport seems to be mirroring the escalating violence in society. Like acts of violence as a result of road rage, violent acts on the sports fields have begun to be adjudicated in courts of law. Parent and spectator behavior on the sports field is often beyond the control and influence of school personnel, league administrators, officials, or coaches.

Action plans for dealing with potentially violent situations can help the coach deal with problems when they arise. The National Alliance for Youth Sports (NAYS), an organization that educates coaches and parents on the needs of young athletes, has researched parental behavior at athletic events (Nack & Lester, 2000). It found that in 1995, you could expect 5 percent of a crowd of parents to get out of line at a youth sport event. This included behavior such as verbally abusing players, coaches, or officials. In 2000, the percentage of out-of-control parents had risen to 15 percent.

Competitiveness

It is up to the school district and coach to determine the level of competitiveness of the team. In an established athletic program, as long as the goals are developmentally appropriate and educationally sound, parents do not have the right to determine the team goals. It is not uncommon for parents to want their child to be on a "winning" team. If winning is not the primary goal of the team, and the goals of the team are established at the preseason meeting, those looking for a more- or less-competitive experience have the option to look for another sports program.

Qualities and Values

The coach who can articulate some of the personal qualities and values that players will learn from being on the team will have an easier time communicating with parents. Effective leaders have a vision, and they create a community with shared values and a common goal to achieve it. Coaches whose vision includes positively influencing players' character will probably find dealing with some parents challenging. The best outcome would be to have parents buy into the coach's vision. However, it may be more realistic to clearly establish the team goals, values, expectations for behavior, rules, and consequences and then ask parents to choose whether this program is the right one for their child.

Sideline Coaches

Some parents coach from the sidelines with good intentions. Parents who give performance or coaching cues usually think they are helping the coach and players. They may not realize that their comments can be distracting, poorly timed, or perceived as criticism. They may also be giving incorrect performance cues. Part of the coach's job is to give the right balance of constructive criticism and positive reinforcement to optimize the players' skill development and self-confidence. Feedback from other sources can change the balance or overload what they can use. Particularly during games, when players' anxiety levels may be high, coaching cues can be counterproductive.

In the case of a parent who is giving controlled, well-intentioned feedback to players, just talking to the parent one-on-one and explaining why it is not helpful may be enough to stop the behavior. At the other extreme is the parent who is totally out of control. Comments, tone of voice, and gestures are all indicators that the parent has the game out of perspective. It is difficult to deal with an irrational parent—particularly in a public situation.

At the minimum, the parent may need help with stress management or in the case of more extreme behavior, perhaps professional help. If there is not a way to speak with the parent privately, and if the behavior is not physically violent, the best solution may be to ignore the behavior and call the parent the following day to set up a meeting. As long as there is no imminent danger, a cooling-off period prior to discussion can be beneficial.

Coaches and the Community

We live in a competitive society, and it is easy to lose sight of who is on our team. Parents who cannot be positive spectators may need to be prevented from coming to games or practices. It is very important that coaches maintain their composure under stressful conditions such as these. Coaches who lose their composure are not really in a good position to talk to players or parents about their lack of self-control.

If the saying "it takes a community to raise a child" is true, then parents, league or school administrators, officials, teachers, and coaches need to work together to help children become the best they can be. Unfortunately, some parents believe that giving their child "an edge" over their peers or covering up for their mistakes is helping them. When parents have a "them-versus-us" mentality, it is difficult for coaches to help their children learn to become the best they can be and contribute constructively to their community.

Special Events

Some coaches have found it helpful to involve parents in special team functions. Having parent-child games, dinners, and special events can be a way to foster positive relationships. Coaches who can get parents to believe in, and support, their philosophy can maximize the influence they have on players' behavior. It is also more likely that the lessons they learn from their team participation will carryover into other areas of their lives. The best chance of getting parents to be part of the community is to let them know that you care about their child and that you are fair. Although no easy feat, once coaches have earned the trust of parents, they are well on their way to realizing their vision for the team.

CHAPTER 8

Is It a Community-Building Initiation Rite or Is It Hazing?

• After being forced to drink 20 shots of whiskey, a Virginia high school softball player passed out and went into a coma.

• At a small private school in New York, players were required to have intercourse with a sheep.

• In an activity also referred to as the elephant walk, lacrosse players at a Massachusetts high school were required to strip from the waist down and walk in a circle holding the genitals of the player in front of them.

• A cheerleading squad from Illinois was asked to simulate sex acts while covered with bleach and other substances.

• In a "butt-burning" incident, male soccer players were suspended for spraying and lighting another player's pants.

• A Connecticut high school wrestler had his head thrust into a toilet and flushed in a ritual known as "swirlies."

Hazing

Hazing is defined as any activity required to join a group that endangers the emotional, psychological, or physical well-being of the participants. Hazing activities include acts that are illegal, sexual, physically dangerous, or involve humiliation or substance abuse. The incidents cited in the text box above are examples of hazing activities because they endanger the well-being of the participants. Some alarming statistics from a national survey on initiation rites among high school students, conducted by Alfred University (Hoover & Pollard, 2000), indicated that 48 percent of the students who belong to groups reported involvement in hazing activities. Of this group, almost 75 percent experienced some kind of negative consequences as a result. A quarter, or 25 percent, reported their first hazing experience before the age of 13. Athletic teams have been reported as one of the groups with the highest incidence of questionable initiation activities. According to the Alfred University study, 80 percent of college athletes reported being subjected to questionable or unacceptable initiation rites.

Initiation rites are usually organized by team members with the most seniority. Often there is a long tradition of bonding experiences and initiation rites that are required for new team members. The nature of the experiences vary widely. Some of them are relatively harmless initiation rites that serve to promote bonding and cohesiveness. Others are humiliating, denigrating, dangerous, or involve illegal activities. When the experiences fall into one of the latter categories, also known as hazing, they are dangerous and in many states illegal.

Team Initiation Rites

Young people have a strong need to belong, and being part of a group is one of the attractions of joining a sport team. In return for group membership, initiation rites are commonly required. The purpose of these rites is to promote group cohesiveness and to facilitate relationships with other group members. Initiation rites also build a sense of community and promote prosocial behaviors and values that identify the group. As induction exercises, initiation rites are a way of ensuring that the norms and values of the group remain intact, as new people join the community. Some initiation rites are community-building activities. Taking an oath, being a part of a mentoring program, or taking part in cooperative games or adventure activities are activities designed to promote trust, cohesiveness, and respect for the safety and well-being of other group members.

What Is Happening On My Team?

Coaching involves much more than the time put in for practices and games, and at the beginning of sport seasons, coaches are especially busy. Because most initiation activities do not take place during practices, it is easy for coaches to overlook or downplay what is happening. Initiation rites are not usually considered official team activities. For this reason, the process is often conducted by senior team members rather than the coach. However, coaches who want to promote positive, trusting, and respectful relationships among team members must provide leadership and guidance during this important process.

The purpose of initiation activities is to define the shared values of the team and to establish the team's identity. Whether initiation rites are positive community-building experiences or dangerous or sadistic hazing is determined by those who design them. A youth or school sport coach who chooses not to be involved in the initiation process is deferring this responsibility to the players. Given the statistics, it is probably not a responsibility that they are developmentally ready to handle without guidance. Research indicates that these experiences often have dramatic and perhaps even life-altering consequences for team members.

Proactive Leadership

Coaches who communicate with their players and take part in planning induction activities can shape their development in a positive direction. There are a number of preventive things coaches can do to discourage hazing. One is to work with the captain and senior members of the team to plan constructive activities. Adventure and cooperative activities can promote trust, respect for the others' safety, responsibility, self-esteem, and cooperation. They are also challenging and enjoyable. This is important, because many students reported that they participated in hazing because it was "fun and exciting" (Hoover & Pollard, 2000). Emphasizing these values through active participation in challenging activities may deter the development of less-constructive ideas. It also focuses on developing positive relationships among the team members. Since many hazing activities are dehumanizing and humiliating, activities that strengthen relationships can be a natural deterrent.

When a coach takes the time to meet with senior team members to develop initiation activities that are constructive and consistent with the team values and goals, then players learn responsible leadership. They are learning how to create an environment that will foster trust, caring, and cohesiveness among the team members. It gives them a positive experience in leadership and decision-making and reinforces the values that are the foundation of the team as a community.

Discussing Initiation

Another preventive measure is discussing initiation rites and hazing activities with the team. Particularly with teams that have a history of questionable initiation activities, it may be beneficial to work with the team leaders before the planning begins. Team discussions about hazing incidents and their destructive effect on trust, respect, and teamwork may help some players put these activities in perspective. Discussing the feelings of victims of these experiences encourages the development of compassion. For others, relating hazing incidents with catastrophic results may help them think differently about the activities. Educating students can empower them to have the courage to walk away from activities that are potentially dangerous, humiliating, or illegal.

It probably is not surprising that players are influenced by adult attitudes toward hazing. The Alfred study also found that students who knew an adult who was hazed were more likely to be hazed themselves. It could be that students who hear stories about coaches' hazing experiences may believe that participation is a necessary right of passage. Thus, coaches' personal experiences with hazing and initiation rights should not be a part of team discussions.

The Alfred University study also found that many students are not clear on what an appropriate initiation activity is and what constitutes hazing. They believe hazing is something that most people experience in exchange for the privilege of belonging to a group. In their drive to belong, players who have not been given a clear negative message about hazing may see this as a signal that they need to conform to be a part of the team. If the coach does not take a strong stand against hazing, players are likely to think they have unspoken approval.

Keeping a Watchful Eye

A coach can pick up a lot of information by listening to the interaction among team members and observing their behavior toward each other. Controlling behaviors are usually easy to identify. Some indicators of hazing activities are that new team members are doing all the menial tasks at practice and that direct orders are being given to new team members by those who are more senior. Also, tradition is often a precursor. Stories of things done in the past can be strong indicators of things to come. Sometimes there is a need to outdo what was done before.

Intervening

Sometimes preventive measures are not successful and intervention is required. Although the coach may not know the details, when indicators point to harmful, destructive, or illegal activity, the coach needs to take action. What action the coach chooses to take will depend on the severity of the problem and the power hierarchy and personalities of the official and unofficial team leaders. One option is to talk to the captains first. Depending on the captains' role in the activities, they may be the most effective liaison to the team. Another option is to start with a meeting of all the senior members of the team, or to hold a meeting with the entire team.

If the problem is extremely serious, a meeting with parents and players may be the most effective way to stop the behavior. Any time a coach is worried enough to choose this option, he or she should discuss it with the athletic director and school principal prior to notifying parents.

There are times when coaches have to step in and make decisions for players. Clearly, their first priority is the safety and well-being of their athletes. Coaches often have to make critical judgment calls regarding the seriousness of a problem. As in the case of the overly aggressive player, young people sometimes need decisions made for them to protect them from errors in judgment that will have long-lasting effects on their lives.

However, there are other times when adults need to guide and shape behavior and allow players to make their own decisions with enough latitude to learn from their experience. Respect for others, self-control, and responsibility are not most effectively learned using a strict obedience model. Therefore, when coaches make decisions for their players, they are overriding the players' involvement in the decision-making process. While it may stop the immediate inappropriate behaviors, it may not aid in the promotion of other outcomes.

Disclosure

A caveat regarding disclosure is important. The tragedy at Columbine High School and the subsequent wave of school shootings and violence have resulted in a demand for tightly controlled supervision and reporting of behaviors that threaten the safety of students. This puts pressure on all school personnel to report and take immediate action under conditions where students threaten each other's safety. School personnel who have chosen not to act or communicate with authorities, when they had knowledge of potentially dangerous situations, can be sued for negligence. When coaches choose a course of action to deal with initiation rites, they need to weigh carefully the potential for harm to students. In instances where coaches are aware of initiation activities or hazing, (particularly in states where hazing is illegal) and they do not disclose their information, they may be found liable in the event of harm to students.

The Big Picture: The Purpose of Athletic Teams

Young people learn about community membership and values through their experiences. The challenge for coaches is to help players understand how their behavior and values define who they are as individuals and as a team. If the coach views the team as an intentional community, the shared values of the group and how team members relate to each other is the litmus test for the team's success.

Belonging is a strong developmental need that does not end after the teenage years. It is a human need throughout life. Being part of a group—whether you are 8, 15, or 50—has inherent challenges. In many groups, unconditional loyalty is often an unspoken requirement for belonging. It is often referred to as the "code of silence." If an inductee questions the required activities or reveals any information about the activities to anyone outside the group, he or she does not pass the test.

As discussed in Chapter 4, the most-difficult decisions often require two core values to be prioritized. In the case of hazing, respect for others is often stacked against loyalty. During hazing activities, loyalty to the group is given higher priority than the safety and welfare of individuals. It also often requires members to be dishonest about their activities. Although the process may increase the cohesiveness of the group, it creates a community based on power and fear rather than trust and respect.

If sport is to be a character-building experience, the values athletes learn need to be positive ones. People with strong character act on principles. Through their experiences, young people learn about values, behavior, and the principles that guide them. Most people consider loyalty a positive quality. It is a value prized by families, political parties, employers, and peer groups. Loyalty can unify a group, but it is a double-edged sword. When loyalty is prioritized over other values such as honesty, caring, and compassion, it can erode the foundation of the shared values of a group. Ironically, hazing activities often undermine their own purpose, which is to create a strong and healthy community.

CHAPTER 9

Sexual Harassment

Which of these situations is sexual harassment?

• Coach Riley is only 22 and coaches the girls' varsity basketball team. In an effort to involve the team in decision-making, he begins to work on new plays after practice with Nancy, the captain. Nancy is an 18 year-old high school senior. She volunteers that a local college is using the same offense their team is working on and suggests they go to see it in action over the weekend. Coach Riley agrees and picks her up at the school on Saturday morning. They attend the college game, stop for lunch, and then return to school and spend the rest of the afternoon fine-tuning the plans for practice the next day.

• Several members of the boys' lacrosse team believe that Greg, the team's center, is gay. They begin to taunt him in the locker room. Graffiti is plastered on his locker, and rumors about his sexual preference are rapidly spreading through the school.

• Tanya is the student athletic trainer for the boys' soccer team. Players on the team begin making suggestive comments about her body. Several team members have told her they want to "get it on with her." Tanya makes it clear that she is not interested. When she arrives at the training room one day, she finds pornographic pin-ups on her office door. She decides to tell the coach she wants to quit her student internship with the team.

What is Sexual Harassment?

Sexual harassment is a term that describes a broad spectrum of unwelcome behaviors that are sexual in nature. Sexual harassment can be defined legally as well as ethically, and the legal and ethical definitions may be different. Specific circumstances and differences in perception often make it difficult to distinguish among behaviors that are considered to be sexual harassment as legally defined and those that are unethical, unprofessional, or just in poor taste. Because sexual harassment covers a broad range of behaviors, it is probably easiest to understand using working definitions and examples. By the end of the chapter, you should be able to determine which of the situations in the text box are examples of sexual harassment.

The Legal Definition of Sexual Harassment

Student athletes of any age are legally protected from sex discrimination by the federal requirements of Title IX of the

Education Amendments of 1972 (Title IX, 2000). While engaged in school-sponsored programs and activities, students are protected on school grounds, at away games, on the bus, at training camps, tournaments, and other locations. One type of sex discrimination is sexual harassment. Legally, there are two forms of conduct that are considered sexual harassment. The first form, *quid pro quo harassment,* means "you do this for me and I'll do that for you." It occurs when a school employee leads a student to believe that he or she must submit to unwelcome sexual conduct in order to participate. This form of sexual harassment can involve unwelcome sexual advances, requests for sexual favors, comments or gestures, or touching of a sexual nature. It can range from subtle sexual innuendos to outright verbal or physical abuse. The second form, *hostile environment harassment*, occurs when unwelcome sexually harassing conduct is persistent, pervasive, and so severe that it affects a student's ability to participate in, or benefit from, the program or activity (U.S. Department of Education OCR, 1997).

Conduct considered sexually harassing includes sexual advances, touching of a sexual nature, graffiti of a sexual nature, displaying or distributing sexually explicit materials, sexual gestures, sexual jokes, pressure for sexual favors, touching oneself sexually or talking about one's sexual activity in front of others, and spreading rumors about or rating students regarding sexual activity or performance. All students and employees are protected against both forms of sexual harassment from school employees, other students, or third parties.

Title IX protection against sex discrimination extends beyond the coach-player relationship. It also includes relationships between athletic directors and athletes, coaches and assistant coaches, athletic directors and coaches, and athletes and athletes.

Coaches as Professionals

Most professions have a code of ethics that provides standards of behavior for good practice. Often the minimum legal standards for professional behavior are below the ethical standards for good practice promulgated by professional organizations. NASPE, the National Association for Sport and Physical Education, has a clearly defined position statement on coach-player relationships and sexual harassment. According to the NASPE position statement (2000): "Sexual and/or romantic relationships should not be tolerated between coaches and athletes. Such relationships are unprofessional and represent an abuse of professional status and power. The nature of the coach/athlete relationship requires that the coach is always responsible for maintaining the professional relationship. Intimacy initiated by the subordinate must be anticipated, discouraged, and avoided by the coach."

One common ethical standard for the helping professions—such as doctors, lawyers, social workers, and psychologists—is to put the needs of the constituent first. Once there is a personal relationship, the boundaries of the professional-constituent relationship become blurred. For this reason, such relationships are viewed as unprofessional and unethical because they affect the professional's objectivity regarding judgments and decisions about the constituent. For coaches, not only will the objectivity regarding an individual player be affected, but their ability to be fair to all team members is also compromised.

Drawing the Line in Relationships With Players

It is not surprising that feelings develop between coaches and players. The very nature of coaching involves spending a great deal of emotionally charged and intense time with players. There is something special about a coach's relationship with players, akin to those of doctor and patient. However, regardless of the age of the player, it is the responsibility of the coach to be sure that the feelings are not acted on and that vulnerable athletes are not exploited. In order to grow and learn, players need to be open to change. This vulnerability requires trust and willingness to take risks. Taking advantage of the trust and vulnerability of athletes is an abuse of power and authority (Lane, 1998). When a relationship develops from coach-player to coach-lover or even coach-friend, the interaction and nature of the relationship is changed.

In addition to problems with objective decision-making, there are power differentials that make relationships between coaches and players inherently unequal. People in authority abuse their power when they use their status as a means of control and persuasion. Even when a player either initiates or consents to a sexual relationship, it is still an abuse of power and status. The coach has the responsibility to maintain the integrity of the professional relationship. Sexual harassment is more about the abuse of authority and power than it is about sex. In the context of the coach-player relationship, ultimately it is a betrayal of trust (Lane, 1998).

Impact on the Team as a Community

Even if a coach who is having a personal relationship with a player is being fair to the team, that may not be the perception of the other players. Negative feelings and mistrust develop when players feel that a coach favors one player over another. Trust, respect, loyalty, and fairness are compromised. These feelings undermine the values of the team as a community.

When coaches define the shared values of their team, boundaries for behavior, and consequences for inappropriate behavior, they are defining their community. To function as a cohesive unit and healthy community, all team members must treat each other respectfully. Players must trust that the coach will reciprocate their trust by being fair and keeping their best interests in the forefront. Once a coach acts on special feelings for an individual player, the stability of the community is irrevocably compromised and the ethical standards for good coaching practice are violated. If the nature of the coach-player relationship falls within the legal definition of sexual harassment, it is not only an ethical breach of practice, it is illegal.

Sexual Harassment Among Teammates

One vital role of the coach is to model and promote respect for others. Participating on a sport team can be a positive environment for learning respect and an appreciation for diversity. However, these are not automatic by-products of competitive sport experiences. The coach has to create and maintain an environment that promotes these values. Team members do not have to be best friends, but they do have to behave respectfully toward each other. Although players may not mean to be disrespectful, jokes and comments that are sexually demeaning or humiliating are forms of sexual harassment. Players need to be made aware of how others may perceive comments, jokes, gestures, or innuendos. Seemly innocent comments can be offensive.

Coaches who overhear jokes or see gestures that are demeaning need to take steps to let players know that the behavior is inappropriate and may even be illegal. Coaches who laugh at sexually explicit jokes, show amusement, or even remain silent when a player engages in behavior that is sexually harassing condone that behavior. Coaches who see disrespectful behavior in general, or sexually harassing behavior specifically, need to address the problem with the player. It is likely that players who are disrespectful to family members, friends, or peers will also have difficulty being respectful toward teammates.

Finally, players need to know what sexual harassment is and how to file a grievance if they find themselves a victim. Coaches who take the time to define and discuss sexual harassment make a statement to their players about expectations for behavior and may discourage sexually harassing behavior before it starts.

Grievance Procedures

According to Title IX, schools are required to adopt and publish a policy statement and grievance procedures for sex discrimination in general; separate procedures for sexual harassment are not legally required. The key elements of the grievance procedure should include notification to students, parents, and employees about the grievance process and with whom the complaint should be filed. All parties should be given a prompt and equitable time frame for each stage of the investigation process and notification of the final outcome. An impartial investigator should be assigned to the case and all parties involved should have the opportunity to present evidence and witnesses. There should also be assurance that the school will correct any discriminatory practices and take steps to prevent future occurrences (Title IX Regulations of the Education Amendments of 1972, 2002).

Discussion

The Coach-Player Relationship

What about Coach Riley's relationship with Nancy? As described in the scenario, the relationship is not sexual. At this point in time, Coach Riley is probably not legally guilty of sexual harassment. However, given the amount of time he and his captain have spent alone together, including a stop for lunch, and the fact that he drove Nancy to the game are red flags for future problems. There is reason to question whether Coach Riley has drawn the appropriate line between his personal and professional relationship with his captain. It does not appear that there have been any ethical breaches of conduct. However, there is reason to question his professional judgment.

Nancy's perception of the special treatment she has received is open to speculation. She may be interpreting their time together as part of her job responsibilities as captain and she may have no thoughts about the coach's personal feelings or motives. On the other hand, she might be attracted to and interested in Coach Riley. She may view their lunch and trip to the college game as signal of his personal interest in her. In her mind, this could have been a "first date." Title IX distinguishes between welcome and unwelcome sexual advances. It is difficult to know what Nancy's feelings are. How does she feel about spending her Saturday with her coach? Is she doing her job as a captain at the coach's request, or is there a personal interest? If she is not interested in the coach, any future sexual advance would be unwelcome and constitute sexual harassment. If future advances are welcome, then the coach may be unprofessional and unethical but it would not be illegal unless the student was under the age of 18.

It is likely that the coach is creating difficulties for the future. In terms of the time spent together, a precedent has been set. Nancy may have expectations that could lead to problems for the coach. Regardless of the motives of the coach, the player's perception of the motives are key. If Coach Riley has no personal interest in his captain, if Nancy is angry, hurt, or humiliated because of her misinterpretation of his interest, false allegations of sexual harassment could result. Or, Nancy may become more flirtatious as a result of her perception of his interest and the coach may have to redefine the boundaries of the relationship.

Coaches can avoid misinterpretations and prevent false allegations by setting and maintaining clear boundaries for their coach-player relationships. Spending time alone, having lunch, and attending outside activities with players are social activities that can easily lead to misinterpretation of interest and intentions.

Harassment Based on Sexual Orientation

In the case of Greg, the allegedly gay player on the lacrosse team, his teammates' behavior falls within the legal definition of hostile environment sexual harassment. Spreading rumors about others' sexual behavior and putting graffiti of a sexual nature on a player's locker are considered sexually harassing conduct. In its revised guidelines, the Office for Civil Rights (OCR) addressed the issue of gender-based harassment such as sex stereotyping. Discrimination that is based on an individual's failure to conform to stereotyped notions of masculinity and femininity may not meet the technical definition of sexual harassment, but it is a form of sex discrimination (U.S. Department of Education OCR, 2001).

Incidents of sexual and nonsexual gender-based harassment may be combined to assess whether a hostile environment exists. In its discussion, the OCR specifically noted that sufficiently serious sexual harassment about sexual orientation may be covered by Title IX, although Title IX does not prohibit discrimination based on sexual orientation. Two key considerations for Title IX applicability are (1) is the harassing behavior specifically limiting or denying an individual the right to participate or benefit from the school's program and (2) does the offensive behavior involve sexual conduct? As case law emerges, the court's interpretation of the OCR guidelines for sexual harassment and sexual orientation will become more clear.

Sport provides an opportunity for individuals from different ethnic, racial, religious, and socioeconomic backgrounds to work together toward a common goal. While working together cooperatively, players can learn to respect and learn about people who are different from themselves. Coaches who believe that respect for others and tolerance for difference are important values will create team expectations for behavior that reflect these values. Whether or not discriminatory behavior is illegal, coaches need to promote players' development of self-esteem, respect for self and others, and self-control. Although coaches may not agree with the beliefs, choices, or lifestyle preferences of their players, discriminating against them or allowing them to be treated disrespectfully would violate professional and ethical standards for good practice. It may also be a legal violation of Title IX Regulations (2002).

Flirtatious Behavior and Sexual Harassment

The situation with Tanya, the student athletic trainer for the boys' soccer team, involves a clear-cut case of sexual harassment. Although some team members may think their behavior is harmless flirtation, it has gone well beyond that. According to Title IX, unwelcome sexual advances toward other students, suggestive sexual comments about her body, and pornographic pictures on an office door are all considered peer sexual harassment. These behaviors create a hostile environment and are in violation of Title IX (U.S. Department of Education OCR, 2001).

Taking immediate effective action may include age-appropriate corrective measures by the coach. Depending on the specific circumstances, the coach may warn or take disciplinary action against the offending players or even suspend them from the team if that is what it takes to modify their behavior. Coaches who are not aware of sexually harassing behavior are not exempt from responsibility for what is happening on their teams.

When Tanya goes to the coach (or head staff athletic trainer) and reports the behavior of the soccer team members, she should be given the name of the Title IX compliance office in the school to whom she can report the incident. It will be the job of the compliance officer to investigate whether the incidents she reports have denied or limited her participation in the athletic training internship program and whether the behavior of her peers is sexually harassing. If the investigation finds that the behavior was harassing and did limit her involvement in the school program, the school must take immediate and effective steps to alleviate the situation and prevent its recurrence.

If the school does not take such steps, the OCR can be asked to investigate. OCR review will determine whether the school disseminated a sex-discrimination policy and effective grievance procedures, appropriately investigated the allegations, and took immediate effective corrective action to alleviate the hostile environment and prevent recurrence. If the school district is found to be in violation of Title IX, it is given the opportunity to comply. If it does not do so, the school district can lose its federal funding (U.S. Department of Education OCR, 2001).

Preventing Sexual Harassment

Sexual harassment claims can be made by anyone in the educational environment at any time. Although more claims are brought against males by females, same-sex claims and claims against females by males are also made. Although there are explicit behaviors that are considered sexually harassing, whether an individual's participation has been denied or limited by it is a judgment call that considers the victim's perception. What is considered a benign comment by one individual may not be considered harmless by someone else.

Eliminating communication of any sexual attitudes or innuendos is a powerful preventive measure. Players are very observant. Coaches who joke, make comments, or even do something as subtle as raising an eyebrow at an attractive individual make an impression on their players. People often take cues for their own behavior from the behavior of those they admire. Without intending to do so, coaches can communicate an attitude or open the door to behaviors that may seem innocent but later escalate out of control.

Coaching often involves physical contact with players. It is generally accepted practice to have physical contact with players while spotting or physically helping players learn skill mechanics. Coaches need to exercise good judgment when working with students physically to be sure the intent of the contact is clear. Players will be less likely to be uncomfortable with or misinterpret the intent of the contact if the coach's demeanor and communication is professional and focused on the athlete's performance.

Coaches who make a positive team climate a priority generally have fewer interpersonal problems on their teams. A key to a positive team climate is an atmosphere of respect for others. It is easy to include examples of sexual harassment as a part of a team discussion about respect for teammates, opponents, and others in general. Players who understand what sexual harassment is, and know the consequences, will be less likely to engage in it. Coaches who communicate procedures for reporting incidence of sexual harassment let their players know they are serious.

Coaches can prevent misinterpretations of their feelings and behavior by being careful about the types of conversations and the amount of time they spend alone with players. Many coaches do not meet with players alone behind closed doors and do not discuss their personal lives or problems. These practices generally discourage players from seeing the coach as a friend or as socially available. When coaches sense that a player may have a crush or be interested in them, documenting any interactions or situations that may later be questioned is generally a good idea. It is also a good idea to let another colleague or the athletic director know about the student's feelings and anything that has transpired that may be questioned later.

Even the most careful professionals can be victims of false claims of sexual harassment that can wreak havoc on their careers. Although it is not fair, even those found innocent of any impropriety have sometimes had difficulty finding or keeping a job after false claims have been made. This is all the more reason to take preventive measures and minimize the risk of false claims.

Summary and Conclusions

One strong argument for the inclusion of athletics as a part of public education is its potential for promoting positive relationships among diverse populations of students who might not otherwise have a reason to interact. In order for it to be a positive experience, coaches need to create and maintain a safe and respectful environment for all participants. Title IX of the Education Amendments of 1972 protects all individuals against sex discrimination that might prevent them from participating in programs that receive federal funds. Sexual harassment is a form of sex discrimination.

Coaches, as professionals, have a responsibility to provide a respectful environment for learning and to create and maintain a positive climate for all individuals. Under Title IX, coaches have a legal obligation to prevent any form of sex discrimination, including sexual harassment, on their teams. Coaches need to be sure that all team members behave respectfully toward others. Any sexually intimidating behavior that limits or denies another individual the right to participate is illegal.

Coaches also need to maintain a professional relationship with their team members. Sexual relationships with players are an abuse of power and authority, regardless of the age of the player. Relationships with players are considered unprofessional and unethical by most professional organizations. When coaches make unwelcome advances or require players to give sexual favors, the behavior is illegal and in violation of Title IX.

CONCLUSION

There are many reasons young people should participate in sports. It is a great way to spend leisure time. It can be fun and it provides a context for socializing with others. The physical benefits of regular exercise are well documented. There is also the potential for unique educational experiences that may not be as easily taught in the classroom. Sport encourages young people to work cooperatively with others, be responsible, trustworthy, dedicated, perseverant, goal-oriented, and respectful. Whether or not sport builds character, it can still be an enjoyable and beneficial way to spend time in a context that is positive and rewarding.

Success in a competitive society is often defined by winning. Success in law, business, and medicine, for example, is measured by profit and loss. Therefore, it isn't surprising that adults who coach often view winning as the measure of their success. This is compounded by the public nature of sport results. In an effort to put points on the scoreboard, it is tempting to make decisions that do not send a message that will help players in the long run. It takes a strong leader to make the best decisions for the long-term when the result is a short-term setback.

Whether sport mirrors society or sport culture shapes society, there is a need to examine what lessons our children are learning in sports. It is not clear whether behaviors learned on the playing field carry over to the participants' lives off the field. But the experience is an educational one, and as such, it needs to meet the standards of any school or community educational program. As leaders, coaches have choices. The nature of players' experiences is shaped by the coach's choices and the values that undergird them. A coach who wants the experience to be positive, fun, and esteem building will make decisions with that intent.

REFERENCES

Bosworth, K. (1995). Caring for others and being cared for: Students talk caring in school. *Phi Delta Kappan, 76*(9), 686-693.

Bredemeier, B., & Shields, D. (1985). Values and violence in sports today. *Psychology Today, 19*(10), 22-25, 28-32.

Bredemeier, B., & Shields, D. (1986). Athletic aggression: An issue of contextual morality. *Sociology of Sport Journal, 3*(1), 15-28.

Brustad, R., Babkes, M., & Smith, A. (2001). Youth in sports psychological considerations. In R. Singer, H. Hausenblas, & C. Janelle (Eds.), *Handbook of Sport Psychology (2nd ed.)* (pp. 604-635). New York: John Wiley & Sons.

Coakley, J. J. (2001). *Sport in society, issues and controversy (7th ed.).* Boston: McGraw-Hill.

Dunnings, E. (1999). *Sport matters: Sociological studies of sport, violence, and civilization.* London: Routledge.

Engelhardt, G. M. (1995). Fighting behavior and winning national hockey league games: A paradox. *Perceptual and Motor Skills, 80,* 416-418.

Gardner, J. W. (1990). *On leadership.* New York: The Free Press.

Goodman, J., Sutton,V., & Harkavy, I. (1995). The effectiveness of family workshops in a middle school setting: Respect and caring make the difference. *Phi Delta Kappan, 76*(9), 694-700.

Goss v. Lopez, 419 U.S. 565 (1975).

Gubacs, K. (1997). "They (teacher educators) told me how to teach forward rolls: They never told me how to handle a scared student:" The role of caring in physical education [Abstract]. *Research Quarterly for Exercise and Sport, 68*(1), A79-A80.

Haller, C. A., & Benowitz, N. L. (2000). Adverse cardiovascular and central nervous system events associated with supplements containing ephedra alkaloids. *New England Journal of Medicine, 343*, 1833-1838.

Hoover, N., & Pollard, N. (2000). *Initiation rites in American high schools: A national survey. Final report.* Alfred University, NY. (ERIC Document Reproduction Service No. ED 445809)

Kidder, R. (1995). *How good people make tough choices: Resolving the dilemmas of ethical living.* New York: Fireside.

Kirby, S., Greaves, L., & Hankivsky, O. (2000). *The dome of silence: Sexual harassment and abuse in sport.* Halifax, Nova Scotia: Fernwood. Kohn, A. (1992). *No contest: The case against competition.* New York: Houghton Mifflin.

Lane, A. J. (1998). "Consensual" relations in the academy: Gender, power, and sexuality, *Academe, 84*(5), 24-31.

Lickona, T. (1991). *Educating for character: How our schools can teach respect and responsibility.* New York: Bantam Books.

Lumpkin, A., Stoll S., & Beller, J. (2002). *Sport ethics: Applications for fair play.* Boston: WCB/McGraw Hill.

McNeely, C. A., Nonnemaker, J. M., & Blum, R. (2002). Promoting school connectedness: Evidence from the national longitudinal study of adolescent health. *Journal of School Health, 72*(4), 138-146.

Messner, M. A. (1992). *Power at play.* Boston: Beacon Press.

Miracle, A., & Rees, R. (1994). *Lessons of the locker room: The myth of school sports.* New York: Prometheus Books.

Nack, W., & Lester, M. (2000). Out of control. *Sports Illustrated, 93*(4), 86-94.

National Association for Sport and Physical Education. (1995). *National standards for athletic coaches.* Reston, VA: Author.

National Association for Sport and Physical Education. (2000). *Sexual harassment in athletic settings.* Reston, VA: Author.

National Institute on Drug Abuse. (2000). *Anabolic steroid abuse.* National Institute on Drug Abuse Research Report Series. Bethesda, MD: National Institute of Health (NIH No. 00-3721).

Orlick, T. (1978). *Winning through cooperation: Competitive insanity, cooperative alternatives.* Washington, DC: Acropolis Press.

Phillips, D. P. (1983). The impact of mass media violence on U.S. homicides. *American Sociological Review, 48*(4), 560-568.

Russell, G. W., Arms R. L., & Bibby, R. W. (1995). Canadians' belief in catharsis. *Social Behavior and Personality, 23,* 223-228.

Sherif, C. (1977). The social context of competition. In D. Landers (Ed.), *Social problems in athletics essays in the sociology of sport* (pp. 18-36). Chicago: University of Illinois Press.

Shields, D., & Bredemeier, B. (1995). *Character development and physical activity.* Champaign, IL: Human Kinetics.

Shields, D., & Bredemeier, B. (2001). Moral development and behavior in sport. In R. Singer, H. Hausenblas, & C. Janelle (Eds.), *Handbook of sport psychology (2nd ed.)* (pp. 585-603). New York: John Wiley & Sons.

Sipes, R. (1996). Sports as control for aggression. In D. S. Eitzen (Ed.), *Sport in contemporary society* (pp. 154-160). New York: St. Martin's Press.

Sipes, R. G. (1975). War, combative sports, and aggression: A preliminary causal model of cultural patterning. In M. A. Nettleship, R. D. Givens, & A. Nettleship (Eds.), *War: Its cause and correlates.* (pp. 749-762). The Hague: Mouton.

Strauch, B. (2003). *The primal teen: What the new discoveries about the teenage brain tell us about our kids.* New York: Doubleday.

Swift, E. M. (1991). Sports in a school curriculum. *Teachers College Record, 92*(3), 425-432.

Timms, N. (1983). *Social work values: An enquiry.* London: Routledge and Kegan Paul.

Title IX of the Education Amendments of 1972, 20 U.S.C. § 1681-1688 (2000).

Title IX Regulations of the Education Amendments of 1972, 34 CFR Part 106. As amended 65 Fed. Reg. § 68050 (2002, Nov. 13).

U.S. Department of Education Office for Civil Rights. (1997). *Sexual harassment: It's not academic.* Retrieved December 15, 2002, from http://www.ed.gov/offices/OCR/docs/ocrshpam.html

U.S. Department of Education Office for Civil Rights. (2001). *Revised sexual harassment guidance: Harassment of students by school employees, other students, or third parties,* Fed Reg. (January 19).

U.S. Olympic Committee. (2003). *Coaching Ethics Code.* Retrieved May 05, 2003 from http://www.usolympicteam.com/education/ethics.pdf.

Wahl, G., Wertheim, L., & Dohrmann, G. (2001). Passion plays. *Sports Illustrated, 95*(10) 58-71.

Weinberger, D. R. (2001, March 10). A brain too young for good judgment. *The New York Times*, A13.

Weinstein, M. D., Smith, M. D., & Wiesenthal, D. L. (1995). Masculinity and hockey violence. *Sex Roles, 33,*(11/12), 831-847.

Weiss, M. (1987). Teaching sportsmanship and values. In V. Seefeldt (Ed.), *Handbook for youth sports coaches* (pp. 136-151). Reston, VA: American Alliance for Health, Physical Education, Recreation and Dance.

Wentzel, K. (1997). Student motivation in middle school: The role of perceived pedagogical caring. *Journal of Educational Psychology, 49*(3), 411-419.

White, P., & Young. (1997). Masculinity, sport and the injury process: A review of Canadian and international evidence. *Avante, 3*(2), 1-30.

Yesalis, C., & Cowart, V. (1998). *The steroids game.* Champaign, IL: Human Kinetics.

Zaichkowsky, L. D., & Baltzell, A. (2001). Arousal and performance. In R. Singer, H. Hausenblas, & C. Janelle (Eds.), *Handbook of sport psychology (2nd ed.)* (pp. 319-339). New York: John Wiley & Sons.

Zarella, J. (2000, July 10). Florida youth league requires parents to learn sportsmanship. *CNN.com.health.* Retrieved November 3, 2001, from http://www5.cnn.com/2000/HEALTH/07/10/kids.sports.parents/

RESOURCES

Published by the National Association for Sport and Physical Education for quality physical education programs:

National Standards for Athletic Coaches (2003), Stock No. 304-10274
Coaching Education: Designing Quality Programs (2001), Stock No. 304-10243
Nutritional Supplements for Athletes (1999), 304-10202
Principles of Safety in Sport & Physical Education (2002), Stock No. 304-10251
Physical Activity & Sport for Secondary School Students (2002), Stock No. 304-10250
Liability & Safety in Physical Education & Sport (2002), Stock No. 304-10252
Teaching Games for Understanding in Physical Education & Sport (2003), Stock No. 304-10266
Beyond Activities: Elementary Volume (2003), Stock No. 304-10265
Beyond Activities: Secondary Volume (2003), Stock No. 304-10268
National Standards for Physical Education, A Guide to Content and Assessment (2003), Stock No. 304-10275
Concepts and Principles of Physical Education: What Every Student Needs to Know (2003), Stock No. 304-10261
National Physical Education Standards in Action (2003), 304-10267
Physical Activity for Children: A Statement of Guidelines (2003), Stock No. 304-10276
Active Start: A Statement of Physical Activity Guidelines for Children Birth to Five Years (2002), Stock No. 304-10254

Appropriate Practice Documents
Appropriate Practice in Movement Programs for Young Children (2000), Stock No. 304-10232
Appropriate Practice for Elementary School Physical Education (2000), Stock No. 304-10230
Appropriate Practice for Middle School Physical Education (2001), Stock No. 304-10248
Appropriate Practice for High School Physical Education (2003), Stock No. 304-10272

Opportunity to Learn Documents

Opportunity to Learn Standards for Elementary Physical Education (2000), Stock No. 304-10242

Physical Education Program Improvement and Self-Study Guides (1998) for Middle School, Stock No. 304-10173, for High School, Stock No. 304-10174

Assessment Series

Assessment in Outdoor Adventure Physical Education (2003), Stock No. 304-10218

Assessing Student Outcomes in Sport Education (2003), Stock No. 304-10219

Video Tools for Teaching Motor Skill Assessment (2002), Stock No. 304-10217

Assessing Heart Rate in Physical Education (2002), Stock No. 304-10214

Authentic Assessment of Physical Activity for High School Students (2002), Stock No. 304-10216

Portfolio Assessment for K-12 Physical Education (2000), Stock No. 304-10213

Elementary Heart Health: Lessons and Assessment (2001), Stock No. 304-10215

Standards-Based Assessment of Student Learning: A Comprehensive Approach (1999), Stock No. 304-10206

Assessment in Games Teaching (1999), Stock No. 304-10212

Assessing Motor Skills in Elementary School Education (1999), Stock No. 304-10207

Assessing and Improving Fitness in Elementary School Physical Education (1999), Stock No. 304-10208

Creating Rubrics for Physical Education (1999), Stock No. 304-10209

Assessing Student Responsibility and Teamwork (1999), Stock No. 304-10210

Preservice Professional Portfolio System (1999), Stock No. 304-10211

Order online at
www.aahperd.org/naspe or call
1-800-321-0789;
Shipping and handling additional.

AAHPERD

National Association for Sport and Physical Education
an association of the
American Alliance for Health, Physical Education, Recreation, and Dance
1900 Association Drive, Reston, Va. 20191, naspe@aahperd.org, 703-476-3410

About the Author

Carol Alberts has an Ed.D. in Curriculum and Instruction with a specialization in school law from St. John's University and a M.S. in Sport Psychology from The Pennsylvania State University. She is an Associate Professor at Hofstra University in teacher education and was Chairperson of the Physical Education and Sport Sciences Department for seven years.

Dr. Alberts has spent her career preparing preprofessionals for careers in teaching and coaching and is a consultant in the area of sport supervision and safety. She has coached at the youth, high school, and collegiate levels. Her sport areas of expertise include gymnastics, soccer, volleyball, aquatics, and downhill skiing.

Carol is a Fellow of the Notre Dame's Mendelson Center for Sport, Character and Community and a folio reviewer for the NASPE National Standards for Athletic Coaches.

Recognizing the potential for teaching positive values and life skills through sport participation, Dr. Alberts has spent the last five years teaching, writing, and speaking about the messages coaches' behavior and decisions send to their athletes.

DATE DUE